# MADE IN
# MONTANA

## DAVID FUQUA

# MADE IN
# MONTANA

By David Fuqua

ISBN: 979-8-218-47437-9

For more information about the author or to order autographed copies, visit DinoDaveAdventures.com.

PRINTED IN THE UNITED STATES OF AMERICA

## DEDICATION

I dedicate this book to all my family, friends and all the good people of Glendive who have all believed in me. Your positive comments are the reason for this book.

## ACKNOWLEDGEMENTS

Thank you to Jamie Crisafulli and the Ranger Review for religiously publishing my articles and to Tracy Dey for first asking me to write an article.

Thank you to my brother Jon Fuqua for all the editing and good ideas. Thank you to Eric Fuqua for always fixing things I break and rescuing me. Thank you to all my students and especially Baylee who all made me feel like family.

Thank you to Jamie McMillan for the great cover photo and for always being ready for a Makoshika State Park adventure. Thank you to Chris Totty who produced that first Dinodave video and showed me what I could be. A big thank you to fellow dinosaur hunter Homer Hickam, who introduced me to Burke Allen and Kevin D. Miller, who did a terrific job publishing and editing. Thank you to Rachel Anderson who did an amazing job with the final edits. And finally, thank you to mom and dad for moving to Glendive and letting me "grow up Glendive".

Made in Montana by Dave Fuqua

## Contents

# SIGN STEALING

Maybe it was too many of Buttrey's, the local grocery store, jelly-filled donuts. Maybe it was all those extra helpings of mom's Ragu Spaghetti. Or maybe it was all the grape Kool-Aid we drank as often as all the 'Oly' cans we would find near the high school alley. Whatever the cause, I was the slowest kid in the school. I was painfully slow. When I ran, it felt like I was running through quicksand with weights around my ankles. It was like a continuous bad dream when a monster is chasing you. I would run and run, but not get anywhere. In the seventh grade, I foolishly tried out for pole vaulting. I would run as fast as I could and plant the pole vault, but my momentum was so slow, I would only rise a couple of feet and then fall backward like a broken catapult. Even Mr. Layman, the Junior High track coach, couldn't hold back his laughter.

That same year was my first year in Babe Ruth baseball. Childish Little League was in the past. This was big time. A thirteen-year-old playing with fourteen- and fifteen-year-olds. My first game was a bit intimidating, but I had one gift—coordination. The ball didn't go very far, but I could make contact. My first at-bat I hit a slow roller to the shortstop. I looked up at first base and it looked like it was in Egypt. It was SO far away! I ran as fast as I could, but I was stuck in a slow-motion bad dream. The shortstop bobbled the ball, waved to his mom in the stands, and played Tic Tac Toe in the dirt with the second baseman. It didn't matter. He had all the time in the world and threw me out by a mile. It was going to be a long year.

My second at-bat I made contact again, and I hit a slow roller to third. I've seen bunts go further, but this was a full swing. I prepared for the twenty-six-mile marathon to first base, running as fast as I could, but I felt like a Volkswagen hauling a piano. As I approached first base, the ball beat me by a mile, but the third baseman overthrew it! Safe! It was my first time being safe in the big leagues. I couldn't have been more excited. I took a cautious two-step lead off first base, but the pitcher had zero interest in me. There was no chance of me stealing second. Coach Riggs then started giving signs to the next batter.

"Oh shoot, signs!" I thought to myself. We never used signs in Little League and now I had to remember what was what. My mind went blank.

All I could remember was arms folded meant 'steal'. Coach then touched his ear, then nose, then elbow, then all four cheeks, then back to his hat. This same routine would become known in the '90s as "The Macarena". Then, at the end of his dance routine, he folded his arms.

"No way! Arms folded? Is he giving me the steal sign? I just got here!" I looked at how far away second base was.

"I'm a dead man. Well, Coach is coach … here goes nothing." The pitcher, not giving me the least bit of attention, threw the ball and I took off running. I was barely halfway to second base when the ball came out of the catcher's hands, but he overthrew the bag to the outfield. What luck! I was safe at second. I looked at Coach and he gave me a very confused look, but since I was safe didn't think too much of it. On the next pitch, the batter stepped out of the box and I looked at Coach for the signs. Coach once again danced The Macarena. When he was done, he once again folded his arms.

"Oh, no! Third base? Not even our best player, Sam Johnson, steals third base? Man … this coach is bold!" I thought to myself as I led off second base. The pitcher threw a ball outside, and I started running. The whole stadium was in shock. As I made my way past the shortstop, everyone had the same thought. The catcher, the pitcher, the third basemen, the loud mom behind the backstop, the announcer, and even the kid waiting to get a foul ball for twenty-five cents at the concession stand all had the same thoughts.

"What's he doing?!"

I was closer to second than I was to third when the catcher got the ball to third base. But the third baseman missed the catch, and the ball hit the bag. It ricocheted into the fence, giving even me time enough to get to third.

"Safe!"

The ump gave a signal. My team's dugout was the dugout next to third base. Everyone yelled at me, "What are you doing? What are you doing!"

Coach Riggs, who was coaching at third base, yelled at me, "What are you doing?!" as I stood dumbfounded.

I was thinking the same thing about him. In a squeaky thirteen-year-old voice, I defended myself.

"You had your arms folded … that's the steal sign, right?"

Coach looked dumbfounded. "You steal ONLY when I fold my arms after I touch my ear! I have to touch my ear first!"

Coach then walked back to his coaching box, shaking his head. Now I wondered if shaking a head was a sign. The very next pitch was a single up the middle and I scored my first run in the big leagues and received zero congratulations. The rest of the game, Coach Riggs kept his hands in his pocket and never folded his arms again. And wouldn't you know, we ended up winning the game by one run. To celebrate, it was jelly donuts                              for                              everyone.

# A REEL FISHING STORY

The rotary phone in our house gave an annoying loud ring. "Wow, someone wants to talk to us!" I thought as I jumped up, eager to untangle the cords, and answered, "Hello?" with the anticipation wondering of who it could be. Answering the phones in those days was such a slot machine. This time, it was my youngest brother Chris's friend Chad.

"Is Chris there?" He asked.

"No, he's at the swimming pool."

"This is Chad. I really want to go fishing. Do you want to go with me?"

My inner tough kid voice on my right shoulder shouted, "Wait, wait, wait. Chad was two brothers down! A twelve-year-old fishing with an eight-year-old? I was way too cool for that. I could hang with my younger brothers' friends who were only two years younger, but four years? That breaks the number one cool kid code!"

But the inner nice kid on my left gave him a smack and said two words. "It's fishing! Just go fishing!"

My inner nice kid voice never could count well. "Alright Chad, I'll come get you in thirty minutes," I said as I dashed over to Super America, the local gas station, to buy some worms.

I arrived at Chad's house and out came a kid who most likely played catcher and would grow up and win state in shot put.

"Where is your new pole?! Didn't you get a new pole for your birthday?" I asked.

Chad's voice cracked and with a sad puppy dog tone said, "I lost it."

"You lost it in one week?" I shot back, "How do you lose a pole in one week?"

I have never talked to this kid directly once in my life until now. He was just a kid who always came over to play He-Man with my youngest brother. But any kid that can lose a fishing pole in one week won my heart. We were two of a kind. Two kids who were born twenty years before Adderall.

Chad said, "Yeah, I don't know what happened. I was just there fishing, I left to go to the bathroom, and when I came back it was gone! My parents were so mad. I cried all week."

So, Chad and I took his old yucky cheap Zebco fishing pole and headed down to the river.

We went to our usual favorite spot. There was a nice hole at the end of the island. I threw my line in and waited and waited. Nothing. This was odd. Usually, I at least catch a stupid bullhead by now. The bullheads were annoying as they always swallowed the hook and poked your fingers with their spines, but it was better than nothing.

"This is odd Chad. Usually, we get something by now. I'm going to reel in to check the worm."

I started reeling in and felt something odd on the line. "I think I got a snag," I said to Chad in the voice my little league coach would speak to me.

"Don't worry, I think I'm going to get it. No wonder we were not catching anything."

I slowly reeled it in. Boy, it sure felt like one strange snag, but it kept reeling in. "Maybe it's a fish? I think it's kind of fighting?" I said as Chad looked on in anticipation.

Finally, the snag showed itself. It was the strangest-looking stick I had ever seen. I reeled in a little closer.

"Is that a fishing pole on my line? Yeah … look Chad, I caught a fishing pole! I don't believe it!"

When Chad saw that pole come out of the water, his eyes grew as big as a twenty-pound carp. Then Chad started jumping up and down and cheering.

"This is one strange kid, it's just a fishing pole," I thought again to myself, but Chad just jumped up and down cheering as loud as he could. Then he gave me a bear hug.

"Easy, buddy," I said to myself. It's just a fishing pole. Then Chad finally spoke.

"It's my pole! It's my fishing pole! I lost it here last week! You caught my birthday present!"

"Really? No way! Here, take it!" I said while giving Chad back his birthday present. Chad then reeled his pole in. It still had fishing line out.

"I think there is something on my line?" Chad said, puzzled. He calmed down now.

"Well, keep reeling!" Chad slowly reeled the line in as the tip of his new pole bent down with flexibility.

"Keep reeling! I think there is something on there!"

Chad kept reeling and sure enough, there at the end of the line was the mythical drum fish! I jumped up and down.

"A drumfish, a drumfish, my first … I mean *our* first … drumfish!"

A drumfish is considered junk by the ordinary fisherman. But to a twelve-year-old in love with the Yellowstone River, I had always heard mythical stories about the drumfish. 'There is ivory in the brains!' my friends said.

I had always wanted to catch one and look for the ivory and because of Chad; I think I caught one! Technically, Chad caught it first, but I still caught it.

We both continued to cheer and jump around. I thought I was too cool to fish with Chad, but we danced on the beach of Yellowstone River like we had won the lottery. We could not believe our luck. If only the drumfish were as lucky as we were, it might still have ivory in its brains.

# BANNING OF THE BOOGEYMAN

"One … two … three … Paper!" I shouted with my open hand on my other hand. My brother had two fingers that resembled scissors in his hand. That's ok, it was best two out of three. This was one of the most important Paper, Rock, Scissors of my seven years on earth. The stakes were high. Whoever won got the top bunk the rest of the school year. I thought I would outsmart him this round because I knew he thought I was going to go rock. But then, what if he knows I know he knew I was going rock? Then he's going to go scissors again because he knows I know what he is going to do. Hmmm … I had better choose rock then. One … two … three … and I slam a fist on the open palm of my other hand resembling a rock. My heart sank. My brother must have known that I was first going to go rock, know that I knew he was then going to go paper, then changed to scissors, but then knew that I knew he was going to go to scissors thus laying down the paper one step ahead of me. I saw my rock with his paper. Fair is fair. He had the top bunk, and I had the bunk next to the boogeyman.

Whoever was the genius that built beds for a seven-year-old with twelve inches of clearance below the bed surely did not know about the natural habitat for a boogeyman. They sometimes lived in closets, especially if it had a door, but only when they were not under your bed. They thrived under the bed! One incredible ability they have adapted through years of natural selection is the ability to move from the closet to under the bed at lightning speeds as soon as the lights are off. My brother climbed up to the top bunk and it shook like an earthquake.

"Ok! You can turn off the lights now!"

"Oh, great … and here goes the other punishment for taking the lower bunk. I had to be the one to turn off the lights," I cursed to myself.

There was about ten feet from the light switch to the bed. Every night was a race between me and the boogeyman in the closet to get to my bed. I flicked the lights off and dashed for the bed and only took two steps, then made a flying leap. I figured if I leaped from a distance, he couldn't grab me from below if he beat me. Every night, I would find the exact distance to the middle of the bed and stay there all night long. It was a nightly ritual. I would listen to the hamster run and run on his wheel while I gave it everything I had not to dangle my hand over the edge.

I had just watched Peter Pan a couple of weeks prior. There was no doubt in my mind that Captain Hook lost his hand by dangling it over the edge of his bed. The Boogeyman loves hands. Feet are ok, but hands are his favorite. I wasn't about to lose a hand. No way, not tonight. Night after night, when the lights were off, I would battle the Boogeyman while the hamster ran and ran on that squeaky wheel. I would lie there in the middle of the bed, afraid to move a muscle until the morning light. Then, one night, I did something different.

"The Boogeyman has to have a weakness," I thought to myself. I started thinking hard.

"I got it!" An idea popped into my head so loud it must have scared the hamster because it stopped running.

"I am going to give myself a force field!" I then imagined a force field all around my body. If the Boogeyman touched this force field, it would shock him immediately. Nothing could touch me with my force field. As soon as I had this field around my whole body, my confidence grew. My hand inched closer and closer to the edge.

"Here goes nothing," I whispered to myself as my hand inched closer to the edge.

My heart rate rose. Then I dangled it like it was a Dukes of Hazzard car dangling from a cliff. I counted to ten. I heard somewhere that sometimes it takes the Boogeyman a few seconds to get the smell. Boy, is he going to get it when he tries to bite through my force field.

One … two … three … four … five. Nothing. So far, so good. Six … seven … eight … nine … ten! I closed my eyes, waiting for a bite! Still … nothing.

"It's working!"

My thoughts cheered loudly to myself. I got braver and dipped my hand further below the bed.

"Come and get it, big boy…"

I even started dangling and waving my hand all the way to the floor. "Where are you?" I said, talking out loud to myself.

"I'm in bed, duh!" my brother from the top bunk replied.

"Oops … that wasn't supposed to be out loud," I thought to myself, but I didn't have time to be embarrassed. I had a Boogeyman to fight. I dangled my hand back and forth like a worm to a Yellowstone catfish. Still nothing.

I got even braver and crawled out of bed quietly, trying not to disturb my brother on the top bunk. With my force field still in place, I crawled under the bed!

"Where are you?"

This time, I kept my thoughts to myself. I looked all around under my bed.

"There is NO Boogeyman! There is NO Boogeyman!" I turned my force field off and dangled my arms and legs off the bed and spread out like a sloth. The hamster started squeaking his wheel again and the more he squeaked, the deeper in sleep I got. There was nothing to fear anymore. There was no Boogeyman.

# A MANNEQUIN STORY

In the summer of 1982, I had a routine. First, I would vacuum for an hour for my dad at Anderson's clothing store. Anderson's was busily located in the middle of an oil boom main street in downtown Glendive. Next, I would take my two dollars earned, run to White Drug to buy a pack of baseball cards, and once again, no Dale Murphy. Then, I'd walk across the street to Hagenston's Hardware. They would always ask if they could help me.

"NOPE!" I'd reply, walking past like a boss, not realizing how annoying an unsupervised ten-year-old must have been that ran his hands in all the bolts, nuts, and screws just because it felt cool.

Then I would skip to Woolworths. Ah … Woolworths was always the highlight. I would head straight to the back where the pets were. My fish tank was already full of ten-cent guppies, and I wasn't allowed to bring any more hamsters home. I do not know anyone who had a happy-ending hamster story. They got out so much, I would just start naming them Houdini.

Finally, I would end my routine with the ten cents I had left over to get the bottled grape or strawberry crush from the F & G pharmacy break room. Pop always tasted better out of the bottle and because it was 1982, that meant pop was good for you as well.

20

The reason I grew up in Glendive Montana was because of my Grandpa Anderson, who started Anderson's clothing store in 1941. My Grandpa passed before I was born, but his store sure extended some advantages to me as a kid.

This one time, in particular, Crazy Days was coming up. Crazy Days in a small-town downtown Glendive for a kid was always exciting. The employees of all the downtown stores would dress up in costumes and sell all their overstock at garage sale prices. Hagenston's Hardware would sell five-dollar grab bags. A brown paper bag full of who knows what. You could not see it until after you bought it. I fell for it every year as I just *had* to see what was in those bags. Every year I would come home with buyer's remorse and a bag full of plumbing gaskets. But *this* year was different. Woolworths was having hamster races! I needed to save up to buy a hamster if I was going to compete. The sleepless nights of an eternal squeaky hamster wheel, my salivating dog, and the wrath of my mom were not part of this equation at the moment. All I wanted was money to buy a hamster for the Woolworths hamster race tomorrow.

I parked my Star Wars banana seat bike behind the store in the alley and came barging in. "Dad! Do you have any work for me to do today? I need a couple of hours' worth."

"Still trying to get Dale Murphy?" he replied.

"Yeah … still haven't got him."

He could see I was eager, so as usual, he made up some work for me.

"I need some things brought up from storage in the basement. Can you do that?" Dad asked.

I gulped. Not the basement. That's where all the dead mannequins are!

"Uh … yeah … sure, I can do that," I sheepishly answered, and Dad wrote a list of things he needed.

Growing up with a clothing store had its advantages, but the price was mannequins. I hated mannequins and always vacuumed way around them and I thought they were looking at me. I also felt they were going to get revenge on me about the time my brother and I snuck into the showroom that faced Main Street after hours. We would both stand there motionless next to a real mannequin until some poor little ol' lady walked by and we would tap the window just after she passed by as a prank. And now, the things Dad needed were in the creepiest basement that resembled a dark torture chamber dungeon in a medieval castle, full of all their unused mannequins. I was now contemplating just how badly I really wanted to win this hamster race.

I took his list and gradually tiptoed to the entrance of the storage basement. To make matters worse, a few weeks ago at a friend's sleepover, we watched Amityville Horror, and I became convinced every basement wall was the gateway to H. E. double hockey sticks. I peeked in, and the musty, mildewy residue hit you first. The walls were rock and in complete darkness. The light switch was always difficult to find. I stepped over my first dead mannequin.

(In my view, the mannequins in the store were alive, and this dungeon was their graveyard.)

Poor thing had no arms. The further I crept in, the further the safety of the light from the store waned. I stepped over another detached head with a wig, sending heebie jeebies up my spine. With my eyes adjusting to the darkness, I felt around for the light switch. By this point, I could only make out shadows of mannequins around me. My heartbeat and anxiety needle were now in the red. Finally, I found the light switch and flicked it on. "AHHHH!!!!" There … right in front of me, no nose! One eye gouged! One arm! A recycled mannequin stared me in the face like a skeleton staring at Indiana Jones as the lightning flashed. I ran out as fast as I could and left Dad's list behind.

"Hey Dad," catching my breath, "I've decided Dale Murphy strikes out too much anyway, but you know how you said since you work at a clothing store, we could always ask you for clothing?"

"Yes, Dave, what do you need?" my dad said, puzzled.

"I never wanted new clothes. I think I might need some new Underoos!"

"Sure Dave, we just got some new Batman's in."

# THE DRAGON'S TOOTH OF YOUTH

"What are we going to do for your fortieth birthday?" My friend Russ asked me as we put our bowling balls away. I recently picked up bowling again because I figured it was the best way to keep my childhood dreams of becoming a professional athlete still alive. The question was tough to accept. The depression of turning forty filled my soul like a deflated black balloon. I was just about to give him a pitiful, self-loathing answer when something happened. It was as if Ponce de Leon woke me up with a splash of his fountain of youth water.

"Wait a minute … I think I have an idea! When planes fly across The International Dateline heading west, they actually lose a day. If they left on Tuesday, they would arrive on a Thursday. What if we crossed the International Dateline on the day of my birthday? We would thus lose that day and I could stay thirty-nine another year? If someone asks me how old I was, I'd just say I've had thirty-nine birthdays!"

Russ's eyes got big, and he jumped up out of his seat.

"Genius! Dave … you're a genius! Where should we go?"

"Well, I've never been to Japan. I think Japan is across the dateline somewhere."

"Done!" Russ replied.

"The even better news is I don't have to buy you a present!"

We called our other travel buddy, Dave, and asked if he wanted to go.

"It didn't matter what country," I said.

He would always say yes. Years earlier, I asked both if they wanted to go to Belize with me. They both gave an enthusiastic "Absolutely!" Then a pause. "What's Belize?"

True to form, Dave thought my Ponce de Leon *Vacation of Youth* idea was brilliant.

He asked his wife - she yelled in the background, "Can we go to Thailand too since we are over there? I've always wanted to ride an elephant."

Russ and I thought that was a great idea also and thus we planned our trip across the international dateline exactly on what would have been my fortieth birthday.

While making my itinerary, I made one more request to Russ.

"Russ, we have to spend 'One Night in Bangkok'!" Anyone who had an 80s childhood will understand, and Russ once again called me a genius. It would be our last stop after Japan and Phuket, Thailand.

Mount Fuji, Tokyo, elephants, noodles, and no birthday cake. So far, not turning forty has been a resounding success. Our last stop before going home was to see the magnificent 'Temple of the Emerald Buddha' in the heart of Bangkok. The red, gold, and green pillars of Thai architecture conjured awe and reverence. Along the outside of the sacred temple gates, several vendors were hoping to lure a passing tourist. I wasn't interested, but then I walked by a particular vendor. He had raggedy clothes and sat between two very large vendors. He only had a few things for sale displayed on a carpet the size of a chess chessboard. It was as if he was a hot dog stand between two Walmarts. The larger vendors barked at me, "Wat Yu Look for! I have here!" they said in broken English, but I ignored them. Something compelled me towards the ragged man with only a few trinkets for sale. Like a Beverly Hills housewife, I got this uncontrolled urge to buy something, and I HAD to buy from this man. There was a rock necklace on his carpet with the name "Dragon's Tooth". If he had named the same rock something like "Monkey Ear" I wouldn't have cared, but I thought Dragon's Tooth was cool, so I asked him how much and I didn't even barter. I was now a proud owner of a necklace called Dragon's Tooth from Thailand. I thanked him with a "Kap Kun Kap!" and walked away when the man did something peculiar. He said some words in Thai, then with a rolled-up paper, tapped the rest of his trinkets one by one and blessed each of his items for sale. He then noticed the curious look in my eye and rather bashfully said in his own broken English, "It da Buddha prayer of money".

I thought about the incredible odds, that some guy from the other side of the world who happened to like rocks and hate birthdays would buy a rock necklace from this man. I thought about his prayer and didn't believe in the Buddha's prayer of money, but it didn't matter. Whether I believed in Christianity, Allah, Buddha, Darwin, or Tae Kwon Do, it just didn't matter. I now realized that I had just become an answer to a prayer. The necklace had a different meaning now. The Dragon's Tooth was no longer a ten-dollar trinket, but an answer to a man's prayer. I now see all my choices and future choices differently. It gave me a feeling and a sense of how everything in this world is connected. Every choice becomes like a rock splashing in a pond, creating ripples that affect the rest of the pond. I felt more at peace turning forty. It was ok to turn forty now. Well, not now, next year, because being thirty-nine again never felt so good.

Genius!

# AN INDEPENDENCE DAY CAROL

Ahhh … the Fourth of July. "Bah Junebug!" You see, I have turned into Scrooge's long-lost distant relative … Uncle Scram. I've lost the Independence Day spirit. I can think of nothing more symbolic to celebrate America than entertaining ourselves with expensive sparks of instant gratification … all made in China. As my once peaceful small town did its best Beirut imitation, I leaned back in my recliner and gazed at my "Get off my lawn!" cross stitch on the wall (ok, I didn't really have that cross stitch, but I kind of wish I did) and closed my eyes hoping to skip another Fourth. "Bah Junebug!" I said again and drifted to sleep as best one would in a war zone.

Then suddenly, the Ghost of Independence Day past entered the room! He looked just like my ninth-grade shop teacher. Only HIS missing fingers were from a short-fused cherry bomb back in '76. With the eyes of a glowing lit punk and fingernails of a burnt snake firework, he spoke to me,

"Dinodave! Where has your Independence Day spirit gone?"

It should have scared me, but I was too busy thinking to myself, "Please don't shake my hand with those missing fingers. It always weirds me out." Anyway, the ghost of Independence Day then showed me the summer of 1982.

He brought me to my tenth birthday party. "Your birthday is at the end of June, for crying out loud! You always got a bag of fireworks for your birthday, and they were always your favorite!"

I stared at myself staring at that plain paper bag. He's right. I loved getting fireworks on my birthday. Every year it was also the same thing. Mom would plead, "Now you wait until the Fourth to light those!" and every year I gave the same response. I gave three Kardashian-sized, "BUT … BUT … BUT … it's my birthday!" No kid gets in trouble on his birthday, and I would immediately run down to the river and light as many as I could until the old guy with the house on the corner and the "Get off my lawn!" cross stitch on his living room wall started yelling at me. Life was simple as a ten-year-old. Since the dawn of man, mankind has searched for Nirvana, self-actualization, fullness of joy, whatever you want to call it. I will tell you now, achieving it involves a ten-year-old boy and a bag of fireworks.

The ghost then brought me to the next year when I had my birthday at our family's cabin outside of Yellowstone Park. Once again, I received another brown bag of fireworks. I hovered near it like Smeagol of Lord the Rings.

"My Precious!"

I had four brothers in the family, who were also after *my precious*. However, Smokey the Bear's "Only you can start forest fires" ads during the commercials of Dukes of Hazard episodes had me well-programmed. A forest surrounded me, and I was doing all I could to wait until the Fourth under supervision this year.

Speaking of fires, there was always a fire going on at our cabin. My grandma visited that year. All five boys and one sister were outside of the cabin playing, and mom, like shoveling snow in a snowstorm, figured this was a good time to clean. She came across a brown paper bag that looked like garbage. With my grandma sitting by the fire getting toasty, my mom threw my plain brown paper bag of fireworks into the fire!

WHIZZZ! ZING! KAPOW! Mom and grandma just treated themselves to the best living room firework display in the history of living room firework shows. Mom was screaming as if the British were coming, and Grandma danced like it was 1929 again. My only regret was that I had missed this greatest Fourth of July show of all time because I was out playing, and now … the Ghost of Independence Day Past had shown it to me. God bless America.

Then the Ghost of Independence Day Present visited. He showed me the text my buddy sent me before I drifted to sleep. It read "I'll be lighting Whistling Bungholes at the house tonight!".

The ghost then brought me to his house. Not only did he have Whistling Bungholes, but he also bought Pink Elephants, Nuclear Sunrises, Hot Flashes, M5s, Bazookas, and even one named The Trump! It was a glorious stash. The ten-year-old inside me was in awe! My buddy must have spent a thousand dollars on something that lasted maybe an hour.

I asked the Ghost of Independence Present, "But … what about all the good we could do with all this blown money?"

He replied, "This is the USA baby, we still do all that too. Now shut up and enjoy the show."

They lit *The Trump*. I yelled out, "You're fired!" Nobody laughed.

Next, the Ghost of Independence Day Future arrived.

"Hey … Why do I only have three fingers?!" I asked. But before he could reply, another text from my buddy woke me up.

*Whistling Bungholes dude! You coming?*

I jumped out of my recliner, ran to my closet, and put on everything I owned that was red, white, and blue. My attitude changed with every boom I once thought was irritating. On this day, each boom results in a reaction that produces awe, wonder, joy, and excitement. In a country that isn't free, those same booms produce reactions of fear, sadness, bloodshed, and heartbreak. I had found my Independence Day spirit once again. "Alexa … play some Toby Keith! I have some Whistling Bungholes to go watch!" God Bless America.

# STURGIS AND STRAWBERRY TRUFFLES

VAROOM! This week, the compensating thunder of Harley motorcycles will fill the Midwest highways as they make their way to Sturgis. Long hair, scraggly beards, bandanas, faded leather, and dark sunglasses, I never considered myself tough enough to drive a Harley. In fact, the only fight I was in was in second grade. Kyle and I swung as hard as we could that January day. As the crowd of sixth graders gathered in a circle and cheered, we both relished our new playground street cred. The best part was that neither of us could feel a thing as we swung our second-grade jabs into each other. With our thick 1980 winter coats, we may as well have been pillow fighting. That was the last tough thing I've done.

Years ago, I owned a Yamaha VMAX. If motorcycles were drinks at the convenience store, the VMAX would be the twenty-ounce Red Bull. Rollercoasters now make me yawn. I used to meet with several rich country club tennis players every week and drove my VMAX to practice. (This is the part where I lose all tough guy credibility whatsoever).

A player who owned several fast-food joints in the state noticed and said, "Hey, I didn't know you drove a motorcycle! I am going to Sturgis next week and have a hotel there if you want to go."

My ears perked. I knew how tough it was to get hotels during bike week in Sturgis. Sturgis was also a bucket list trip for me. I had to go at least once. I agreed immediately. "C'mon and bring your bike by in the morning and we can load it in the trailer."

Ok, time out … time out! There are rules I live by. I don't wear a shirt with the same band to their own concert and I don't cry at the movies when on a date (Toy Story 3 doesn't count). I don't eat strawberries from Jose at the beach in Cancun (anymore) and I surely will not trailer my motorcycle to the biggest bike rally in the world!

In my best Easy Rider voice, I replied, "This guy rides his motorcycle to rallies. I'll meet you there. Where are you staying?"

My rich country club tennis buddy replied, "At the Sunnyhill Bed and Breakfast!"

Ok, time out … time out! This was my one chance to be a tough guy. There was absolutely no way in Hell's Angels that I was going to stay at a sissy bed-and-breakfast at my first bike rally! I took my voice down another octave and put on my ten-dollar shades without a smile.

"We'll see about that."

Then I took off towards the candy store to get my first fake tattoo. I hoped peeling it off wasn't going to hurt.

Like a lone wolf, I headed to South Dakota from Montana on my own. My rocket VMAX wasn't exactly built for long-distance comfort. I had to put an extra cushion on my seat and pull over every hundred miles to walk off my aching, vibrating rear end. My attempted tough-guy image has now somehow dropped between a florist and a librarian. I noticed all bikers waved to each other. However, there was a direct correlation between the amount that your hand moves and how cool you are. I had to actually practice my wave. At first, it was like Gomer Pyle. I think I saw a couple face palms in my rearview mirror. I eventually got my wave down to just a couple of fingers raised in the air. Just enough to say that I care, but not really. I then bought a bandana with skulls on it. Only a hundred miles to go and my tough guy stock was on the rise again. Now, how to get out of this bed-and-breakfast thing? There was absolutely, positively, no way this rebel soul would stay in some sissy bed-and-breakfast.

The next morning, I had the most exquisite strawberry truffle of my life. The savory cream had the most elegant consistency with the fluffy shortcake and perfectly ripened strawbe … wait, time out … time out! My tough-guy stock dropped again, but I felt sorry for every Hell's Angel who didn't stay in a bed-and-breakfast that night. The guy sitting next to me at the breakfast table looked like he had already done ten years. He dressed like he came straight from the set of Sons of Anarchy. He should have been snorting strawberry truffles, not eating them. Turned out he was the nicest accountant from London and had never ridden a bike before. My tough-guy stock further plummeted.

Sturgis has become more of a tourist attraction than a bike rally now. Filled with wannabe posers like myself, the guy from London, my tennis buddy, and other lawyers and doctors who 'trailered' their bikes from wherever. Even so, it had its share of the real deal. I found this out at the gas station. It was a battle to gas up. Like the runt of the litter, I kept trying to squeeze in, only to be pushed out by someone who had been arrested ten times more than me. This dude with mirrored shades just pointed at me with a glare and moved in when it was clearly my turn. What was I going to do, challenge him to a tennis match?

I eventually filled my tank and headed for the highway. Then, from nowhere, these punks in a Volvo cut me off and almost sent me crashing, but I swerved just in time!

"Gol darn it!" I mumbled under my breath.

I'm usually pretty mad when I say the "D" word. Then, from nowhere, the same guy who pointed at me and stole my spot in the gas line came zooming right next to the Volvo! He rode inches to their window, pointed right in their face, and cursed up a storm! He actually went to bat for me! I now had the courage of a barking Chihuahua to a mailman. I rode the leather coattails of my new tough guy friend and gave Mr. Volvo my own quick king-of-the-road stare and then accelerated away like a boss. Where's Kyle?! This tough guy is ready for my second-grade fight rematch!

# A BRAND NEW MONTANAN

I was born in Montana. I lived most of my life in Montana. My driver's license headlines Montana. Yet … something was missing. It was as if I was Cooper Manning, the brother of Peyton and Eli, who didn't quarterback. Or that I was in an amazing orchestra, but I played the triangle. I called myself a Montanan, but I never really felt Montanan until last week when I was invited to attend my first branding.

In a state where cows outnumber humans two to one, I admit, I've always had a bit of a bovine phobia—with good reason too. Cows killed five times as many people in 2018 as Sharks did. Steven Spielberg missed the mark with Jaws. Make a thriller called "Moos!" and that's the moo-vie that will keep me up at night. I can see the plot now; there I am hiking or on my motorcycle and this beast will not move, just staring … staring blankly at me like my first day of calculus. Why won't you mooooove?

Anyway, the only thing I understand about the cattle world is that they taste good. But I've grown up with friends whose way of life is cattle. They do these things called rodeos. I went to my first one a few years ago in Las Vegas thanks to a free ticket (I can't wait to go to another one for the sole reason of yelling, "Hey Buddy! This isn't my first rodeo!"). At this rodeo, for fun, these guys would strap a rope around the "oysters" of a big ol nasty bull just to make it mad. Logical. Then these guys would get on and ride them for a few seconds. The madder the bull, the better. Hmmm … even more logical. Then a clown would appear from the barrel like David Copperfield and play with these raging bulls like they were cocker spaniels at the dog park. Makes complete sense. This is what happens when you grow up without cable. Needless to say, I was naïve to the cowboy way, but in some sort of Tom Sawyerian way, I was excited to attend my first branding—finally. I feel like Montana should have a check mark on their driver's license right between Motorcycle Endorsement and Organ Donor that says, "Have you branded?". Then, once 'branded' is checked, the word 'REAL' magically appears before Montana.

I showed up in my baseball hat and tennis shoes. I felt like a geeky freshman walking into a seniors-only party. There were cowboy hats, wranglers, boots, horses … this was the real deal. I felt even more out of place. There were even old guys wearing chaps. CHAPS! I didn't know anyone really wore chaps except for that Halloween back in college in my third sophomore year. I wandered off to where the cows were. At this point, I felt I had more in common with them. When I arrived, the calves were already separated, and they were as nervous as I was. I've never heard that much mooing since that annoying "What does the cow say?" toy in kindergarten.

The crowd moved from lunch to the corral and I took my place on the fence, doing my best cowboy pose with both arms over the rails, with one leg slightly bent and a little snarl. I saw it in a country music video one time and I still had no clue how everything worked. I kept hearing the word "wrestle," pronounced "wrassle" if you were over fifty.

In my mind, I was thinking, "Ok, if I go for the hind leg I could get a couple of points for a takedown, then put the little bugger in a half nelson. With a little luck I can get the calf pinned on his back in a respectable time Coach Zody would be proud of." Then … in a flash, they opened the gates and real cowboys on horses started roping these things just like that first rodeo in Las Vegas I went to. The little girl to the left of me got excited and said, "Hey do you want to wrestle with me?"

"NO! You do not want ME to wrestle a calf with you," I replied.

I hadn't even seen it done before and I felt out of place enough. Now I had to have this little girl showing me up. I saw calves dragged out of the pen by a lasso three at a time. Each calf had the same expression I made after my sixth sit-up. Eyes bulging with the tongue out. The little girl to the left of me jumped on that calf with a smile like she was about to get on the tilt-a-whirl. I had the wrestling thing all wrong in my mind. These guys did things fast. My expression was still wonder, awe, and a little baffled when someone yelled to me, "You're next!"

"What do I do? What do I do?"

I felt like I was on a NASCAR pit crew who hadn't even changed a tire before. If the little girl can do it, so can I. PJ - another newbie - had the hind legs. I had the front with my knee on the neck and I thought it was cool that this was a technique that has probably been around for hundreds of years. Later, I learned they gave me the easier job. I'm ok with that. That little doggy was no match for me, as his ancestors are responsible for the few extra pounds I needed to hold him down. I could feel my baseball cap gradually turn to a Stetson as the singe and stink from the blazing hot brand dissipated. I did it and I'm officially a Montanan. Next, my rancher buddy invited me to another event called "insemination." I'm not sure what that is, but if it's as fun as branding, count me in! I think this cowboy thing is something I could get the hang of!

# GETTING BEAR FOR A
# BACHELOR PARTY

Ryan was a childhood friend and college roommate. Shortly after he graduated, he came home and told us he was engaged to his high school sweetheart. We were proud of him, and he made a brilliant choice, as they are both still happily married with who knows how many kids. Anyway ... Ryan had one last request. Not a bachelor party in the worldly sense, but he wanted to do one more guy thing. Some type of guy adventure. What we came up with is that we would take our motorcycles, ride as far as we could away from Bozeman and whenever it got dark, THAT is where we would camp. The goal was to get completely in the middle of nowhere as possible. I loved the idea and sounded like my type of bachelor's party. The day came, and we loaded our backpacks with camping gear and took off on our old Hondas.

We started from Hyalite Canyon, and it wasn't long before we had no idea where we were. Remember, this was before the GPS days and this was just the adventure we were looking for. We made our way through some treacherous switchbacks, made a couple hunters mad, and continued into the unknown trail blinded by the dense forest around us. Ryan and Dave had the same ring to it as Lewis and Clark. Everything was how we imagined except ... my motorcycle had its chain come off often. I would have to stop every so often and put it back on. It only took a minute, but it was very annoying. My bike was older, and I didn't do it any favors on how I treated it. It was an XL which was an enduro built for the streets, but I would always take it where it didn't belong. Hence, it was pretty beat up. Despite the chain glitch, we rode for a good four hours. We were completely lost. Our goal was to get as far away from Bozeman as possible, and it was going splendidly. The sun was setting, and we were now looking for a nice flat place to camp before dark. Just a little further, and a little further … nothing … and it was getting darker.

Finally, we got to the end of the trailhead where we thought we could camp and there was a sign! The sign said, Bozeman, and it pointed with an arrow, *One-Quarter Mile*.

"What! Only a quarter mile!"

We drove for four hours … "How could this be?" Our hearts sank. It was now dark and somehow, we did a giant circle and ended up right back in Bozeman. It was the exact opposite of what we wanted to do. We ended up at Bear Canyon Road, which is just outside of Bozeman.

"Well, we could go home, or just go up Bear Canyon in the dark a ways … make the best of it."

But my chain was getting worse and worse. The stops between putting it on more and more. We just couldn't stop now and pressed on. Going home was not an option. We drove up the canyon in the dark about half a mile and my chain came off twice. I couldn't take it anymore.

I said, "Ryan … if we are going to make it, I have to stop and tighten this."

So, we stopped in the darkest black of the night. Ryan shined his headlight on my chain and tire so that I could tighten it enough to get us to where we needed to go. It was dead calm. I remained focused on my chain when Ryan said, "What's that?"

I said, "What's what?"

He replied, "I think I heard something, like some rustling."

I stopped working on my chain and got up as Ryan started creeping a little closer to the rustling as if he was in a Scooby Doo cartoon.

I was still a couple of steps behind when suddenly Ryan yelled, "Bear!". I knew by his expression that he was serious.

"Bear!" He yelled again and by this time he had already turned around and was two steps past me the other way. I had no choice but to follow him. Now, the key to not getting eaten by a bear is not to be faster than the bear ... but to be faster than the people you are with. Ryan had a track scholarship for the 400-yard hurdles for Montana State. This was not good news for me.

Ryan ran to the nearest tree, and I followed. He started climbing, and maybe it just felt like slow motion under the circumstances, but if tree climbing was a track event, Ryan could kiss that scholarship goodbye. In the back of my mind, I was waiting for a bite out of my butt as I climbed and pushed Ryan up that tree. We both made it about ten feet up and felt lucky to be alive ... for now. I never saw what Ryan saw, but obviously, I was going to take his word for it.

Now what? We were both ten feet up a tree in complete darkness with a bear in the vicinity. We waited.

"Hey Ryan, Can I tell your wife how BARE you got at our bachelor party?" Ryan didn't laugh.

We waited more. Eventually, we didn't see or hear anything anymore. We crept up to the bike. I made sure I had a half-step jump on Ryan toward the tree this time. We started the engine and then revved it as loud as we could to scare it away—hopefully.

With undaunted courage, we drove for about a hundred yards further when we saw fresh tracks! We knew it was from the culprit. We stopped again and showed the flashlight on the tracks. Like a horror movie, we slowly followed the tracks with the light a few more feet when there it was! The culprit in those same tracks! The same beast that forced us into a tree!

We shined the flashlight directly in its eyes and the ghastly beast fearlessly stared back at us only ten feet away. There, down Bear Canyon Road, in the darkest hour of the night, we stood face to face with a mighty BIG!! ... BLACK!!! ... Angus cow. Yes ... we got treed by a cow. Like most guys and bachelor parties, we vowed never to tell anyone what happened that night. I guess I keep secrets about as well as I can run from bears.

# FAKE FIGHTS MAKE GREAT FRIENDS

"You can't be serious!" I yelled in my most fearsome eight-year-old McEnroe voice. "That ball was on the line!"

It was a chilly February morning on the playground that day. There was an old tennis court where we invented our own rules with a kickball. The bragging stakes were high for whoever won. The game was tied. Kyle hit a nice shot, and the ball came down near the snow-dusted line. Kyle saw it differently. "Are you blind? That was easily out!"

I snapped back, and we both argued as the cold fog from our mouths resembled a boiling teapot from our tempers.

"Out! … In! … Out! … In!" We continued to banter as the game stopped and our friends formed a circle around us. It was a vital point. I wasn't about to give in. Suddenly, someone from the surrounding circle yelled, "Fight!"

Wait, what? Fight? I was only eight years old and I had never been in a fight. I didn't want to fight, and I could see in Kyle's eyes he felt the same. A fight was next level, but no one was winning the argument either. Then other kids started chanting, "Fight! Fight! Fight!" there was no backing out now. Backing out of a fight would be worse than losing the game of kickball. Kyle and I both stopped arguing at his point. With the circle of friends chanting, there was no way out for either of us. We stared at each other like two Old West gunfighters with their hands on the holster, waiting for the first to draw.

Our friends kept chanting, "Fight! Fight! Fight!" Then Kyle did the unthinkable. The ultimate sign of grade school disrespect. In my mind, it was in slow motion, but with a quick jab, he knocked the kickball out of my hands. Nobody knocks a kickball out of Dave Fuqua's hands and gets away with it. I stood there in all my forty-five-pound, eight-year-old glory with oversized mittens and a thick winter coat that made me look like the Michelin man. My parents ran a clothing store. I was always warm in the winter. Kyle had the same winter gear. He looked like Randy from "The Christmas Story". I reached back with those mittens, swung as hard as I could and hit Kyle square in the shoulder. Even though it felt exactly like when I punched my Star Wars pillow at home, I still thought, "Oh, that had to hurt!". Kyle didn't budge. "This guy is tough!"

Then Kyle swung a punch at me, right in the gut. I didn't feel a thing. What am I? Superman? This fighting thing wasn't so bad. I swung back, hitting Kyle again in his thick winter coat. He didn't feel a thing.

By this time, our crowd of friends started getting louder, cheering us both on. Suddenly, Kyle and I both forgot what we were arguing about and realized the street cred we were getting. We both swung a couple more punches into our winter coats, which absorbed the second-grade muscles like a marshmallow. Only none of our friends knew we couldn't feel anything. Only Kyle and I knew. I looked at the crowd gathering. The commotion of our circle of friends now drew in sixth graders. "Sixth graders!" I thought. "Kickball? What's kickball? What were we even fighting about?" None of that mattered anymore. My brother and his friends were watching. I'm a star now and swung another punch into the marshmallow abyss of Kyles's coat and I couldn't believe we had sixth-graders cheering for us. I am sure Kyle thought the same thing, and we somehow had this mutual understanding now. No headshots and this was all about the glory, not who was right or wrong anymore.

We could have gone on all day but then someone yelled, "Teacher!" and everyone dispersed like cockroaches when the lights turned on. We didn't get caught and shortly the whistle blew to go inside.

As we both put our heavy coats up in the closet in the classroom, I whispered, "Hey, did you feel anything?"

"No. How about you?" Kyle asked.

"No nothing. What do we tell people? Should we just call it a tie and tell everyone it hurt?"

"Deal!"

Our friends wanted us to continue the fight after school, but we gave high fives to the sixth-graders and talked about the Atlanta Braves, Blondie, and the roller-skating rink on the way home. We would hang out as great friends throughout our time at Washington School for the next several years and vowed never to argue in the summertime.

# GANG LIFE OF GLENDIVE

"So, you going to do this or not?!" Brian said to me with his best ten-year-old Clint Eastwood voice. It was hard to see his face through the glare of the streetlights. Streetlights! I should be home now; it was our only rule in 1982, Glendive. Brian (the names have been changed to protect the guilty) sat there on his Mongoose BMX bike with one foot on the high pedal, handlebars facing him, spitting out a wad of Big-League bubble-gum chew. I sat there on my Star Wars banana seat bike, as I could never afford the gold standard Mongoose. At least it wasn't a girl's bike, with the middle bar between the seat and the handlebars low. It makes perfect sense that a boy's bike should have the steel bar four inches below a tiny seat that will put any kid who can clear two of his friends off a ramp directly into the alto section of the boys' choir upon landing. Cory had a Dallas Cowboys bike. I was insanely jealous but happy he sold me the hand-me-down Star Wars bike. Cory's reputation was on the line now too, as he vouched for me. Cory reinforced the leader, Brian, "Let's go, Dave, are you in?"

"What do I have to do?" I answered in my most tough kid voice, but I was shaking inside. The BMX bike gangs of Glendive neighborhoods were tough. I heard stories. Forest Park Kids could sell you any amount of UPS tire chromies you need. (Those were metal nozzles that went on the air intake of the tires for the 80s kid lingo impaired). The Hillcrest kids' parents drove them everywhere, so they didn't have a gang, but there was the South Side across the tracks. We don't talk about the South Side. I was happy to be with the Heights gang. It was a big moment. I could either face the wrath of not being home by the streetlights or be accepted by the Heights gang forever. I weighed my options. My mom had six kids and already forgot me at a McDonald's once. I didn't think she would notice; I took the chance.

Brian stared at me stone-faced and paused. I could tell he didn't want a ten-year-old in his gang, but Cory vouched for me. I think he also wanted a banana seat in his gang. If someone went down, the banana seats gave the best rides. My mind raced with all the things I might have to do. Pick a fight with a South Sider? I would get pummeled. Steal candy bars at the gas station? I could just buy them and say I stole them. What about knocking on a door and running? Oh, please pick that. I could do that all night.

The gang had all five bikes in a semi-circle pointed at me in the middle. It was the moment of truth as all were quiet, waiting for Brian to utter his verdict.

"My neighbor, Mr. Hawthorne, has a garden," Brian said as he spit out some more Big-League Chew.

"You raid his garden for carrots, and you are in the gang."

The eyes of the semi-circle grew wide-eyed. They knew how mean Mr. Hawthorne was. But in my mind, there was a cloud of confusion. "Carrots? These guys want carrots?!" I thought to myself. I've seen them throw away their carrots a hundred times at school. Do I even feel bad about raiding carrots? I mean, sure, he spent hours watering and perhaps a hundred dollars on fertilizer, soil, and tools for something he could get for 39 cents at Buttery's, but who cares about carrots?

I tried not to laugh. "Okaaayyyy. I'll get you some carrots." There is no way I am going to tell any South-Side kids about this. We then rode past the park to Mr. Hawthorne's, not single file but using the whole road, just like we saw the Hell's Angels do in last week's CHIPs TV episode. The five gang members hid in the bushes, giggling as I walked over to hop the fence. I gave them a "Shhhh!" but they still giggled. I jumped the fence and made my way to the carrot row, or so I thought, and pulled up on the greens. It was a radish. Ew … if this gang wanted any radishes, I would have quit on the spot. I then made my way over to the carrots and quietly plucked a few away by the alley streetlight when Cory giggled too loud. Suddenly, the porch lights flicked on. Five boys jumped from the bushes and scurried to their bikes like cockroaches on the kitchen floor. I stood there like a deer in headlights when Cory yelled, "Run!".

"Hey you kids! Get back here!" The mean Mr. Hawthorne yelled.

I did my best ninja move and jumped the fence, ripping my new 501 jeans before ripped 501s were cool.

Still, it was a successful getaway. We all decided that was enough for the night and I rode home feeling good about my new status at school. Mom gave me a scolding and the grounding I deserved.

"And another thing! You are not going anywhere tomorrow and you will eat dinner with the family!" "Can we have carrots?" I asked. Confused, she could tell by my look that I wasn't just smarting off. "Carrots? We don't even have any carrots!" She replied. I answered back. "Actually … I think you do."

# HOW TO SURVIVE THIRTY BELOW IN GLENDIVE

I survived by doing two things. First, I bought a heat dish. Not a space heater, that's Little League, but a radiant heat dish that you would see at Pet Smart aimed at those cold-blooded lizards. All those lizards do is just eat crickets all day and stay warm. That was my exact goal, and I've always said, "If you want to be successful in life, keep your goals low," and I aimed to be successful these last thirty below days. So, just how cold did it get in Glendive these last few days? It was so cold; my heat bill was actually higher than my Glendive water bill. Ok, that joke was for me, and "if you know you know". But it was so cold, my washing machine pipes froze, so I had to take my human lizard lamp and set it under my crawl space instead of pointing it at me as if I was a two-hour old hot dog at a gas station. Brutal, but at least my blankets were washed.

Now the second thing I did was set my personal best at spending the most money ever for food at a grocery store. That even includes the times I bought just three items at Costco. A high food bill is easier to do these days, and this is for a single guy, mind you. I spent two hundred and twelve dollars! It was glorious. If I had even a hint of hunger, I would open that fridge and I didn't have to just sit and stare at it as usual.

The food was jumping out at me. Comforting food. Like, if I were a bear trying to get as fat as I could before I hibernate through the winter.

For example, let me first share with you a couple of life hacks. Small towns, especially Glendive, are judged based on the amount of national fast-food restaurants we have. This has become the American small-town standard. For those that complain about no fast-food restaurants, I am going to share a couple of secrets so you can have the next best thing. You see … our local grocery store carries Taco Bell hot sauce and Taco Bell taco seasoning. Make sure you buy the "extra, extra" cheap hamburger for the most authentic experience, and BOOM! You too can have Taco Bell right here at home. Don't squeeze the Charmin.

They also sell Arby's curly fries! And I found Arby's sauce right here at our local store. I just put a bag of those in my new "air, fat fryer" and some thin-cut roast beef on a bun. And just for that extra drive-through experience, I used too much sauce and smooshed it flat really good. Authentic. And I didn't even have to scrounge the bottom of a paper bag for those extra curly fries like I was a character from Breaking Bad.

Now, if you are craving McDonald's, all you have to do is grab some of those left-over Amazon cardboard boxes, and if you have one of those fancy Ninja blenders, Voilà! Actually, I'm kidding about that one. What I said was blasphemy. I absolutely love McDonald's. Just buy a couple dozen hamburgers off the dollar menu and store them on top of your fridge. It's ok, they have a shelf life of three to four months. Must be all the preservatives.

So, there you have it, a quick footnote in Dinodave's survival guide to getting through a Glendive thirty below winter. By the way, the secret ingredients to Potato Ole's from Taco Johns are Lawry's Seasoned Salt, cayenne pepper, paprika, and cumin.

You're welcome.

# BE A WILDFLOWER

The beauty of the badlands is best seen at a distance. The closer the view, the blander it becomes—barren and boring. But somehow, the further the perspective of the random browns of the individual sandstone rock blend to a mosaic that feels of design. I was shimmying up some badland hills one day looking for dinosaur bones. There is a feeling of being the first human ever to see a rare dinosaur bone that is addicting. It is the purest form of truth to be the first to unearth something locked up for millions of years. But, on this particular hike, something else caught my attention. The buzzards circled overhead as I walked over a land that the Lakota called "Mako Sica" or bad earth. The usual dominant species were dry weeds or thistles that got caught on my laces. If I was lucky, I would also be without a cactus thorn in my boot by the end of the day. Instead, I came across the most beautiful wildflower that had somehow sprouted in the most torrid of sand and soil.

I had just visited a friend's house with the most perfect garden. My friend provided the perfect soil. He watered every day and got rid of the weeds. The flowers grew vibrant. How could they not be in those amazing conditions? Here in front of me was a flower just as beautiful, but in the most brutal of conditions. I wondered how. I stared again at the wildflower. One flower changed the entire landscape. A bright purple and blue like a lighthouse among a sea of earthy browns and grays. All the wildflower needed was just a little water, just a little. Anything could grow in my friend's garden. That was easy, but none of those seeds could stand a chance out here in the badlands. But the wildflower? All it needed was just a little water.

Two years ago (out of desperation) I was hired as a science teacher. As I'm teaching, I love bursting into random stories about different adventures I've had around the world, but I dare say teaching might trump them all. In my first year of teaching, I was giving a lesson on the history of the geological world. Our earth is divided into geological Eras and Periods marked by significant events such as an asteroid impact or extinction. I then made a timeline of my life on the whiteboard to simulate the Earth's timeline. It was marked mostly by happy events such as "1980 I got a Green Machine; in 1990 I went to college or in 2008 I went to Belize, etc."

I assigned the students to make timelines of their own lives. I expected mostly happy events such as "I got a PlayStation for Christmas in 2008" or "I got a new puppy in 2006".

Instead, to my shock, it was very few of the sort! A fair amount of my students' timelines were burdened with tragedies and not happy events. They were tough to read. Here in front of me were all these amazing kids growing up in the most brutal conditions. Still, daily they demonstrate such persistence and resiliency. Their faces showed a vibrant countenance while the Lakota would call the home they came from "Mako Sica!". I wondered how. Then I thought of that wildflower I came across in the badlands. That's how they are so resilient! I have a classroom of wildflowers. All they need is a little water.

# REFFING FOR MY LIFE

I lost my house. My car. My business. I lost everything. I was a victim of the 2008 housing crash. With what money I had left, I bought an old Isuzu Rodeo and headed to North Dakota as if I were a penniless 49er heading to the California gold. The oil fields of North Dakota had just discovered fracking, and that's where the work was. Luckily, I had some good friends there, so I had a place to stay and just enough gas money to get there.

"Hey, if you need some quick money, they desperately need some refs at the Blue Hawk basketball tournament." My friend told me as I unpacked. "Twenty bucks a game and there are about ten games each day!"

When a friend says the words "Quick money," that's usually trouble, but this sounded great. I played basketball all my life and refereed a couple of church basketball games before. How hard could this be? Four-hundred dollars would save my butt.

That next morning, I was so excited to make some money. The best part was I could watch basketball all day and get paid for it. It was going to be a great day for a brand-new start in my life. They lent me a zebra shirt and a whistle. Two men who looked like they dribbled more oil on their clothes than they ever dribbled a basketball came to the half court for the jump ball.

"This was going to be the most perfectly placed jump ball North Dakota has ever seen," I said to myself, walking to center court. This was going to be such a great day! I threw the ball up with both hands and it wasn't even close to a straight line. The blue team easily won the jump ball.

"What the H--- was that!" The red team yelled at me. It took half a second to receive my first verbal abuse. The oil brutes were so physical, I could hardly tell what was a foul and what wasn't with them. "C'mon Ref!" as they told me places to put my head and there were even more fouls in their language. To make things worse, I felt like I had forgotten everything about basketball. The only good quality I had in that game was that I was consistent. Consistently bad. By the end of that first game, my enthusiasm wilted like a Dakota Sunflower in the winter. Somehow, I made it to the final buzzer, but the buzzer didn't end the abuses as the losing team continued to tell me I was the worst ref they had ever seen. I wanted to tell them they missed more baskets than I did calls, but I had nine more games to go! "Wait, nine games?" I wanted to cry. But they truly were desperate for refs. Nobody else would do it, and I was truly desperate for money.

The day went on and the abuses went on. Occasionally I would get one player who would say, "I used to ref too buddy, I know how tough it is." It was good to hear. I think it should be a rule, that before anyone criticizes a ref in any sport, they should have to do it first.

Finally, after ten hours of reffing, my legs and feet were shaking like the rim after a Shaq dunk. But that was the easy part. I was in a strange new land in which I knew few people and they all verbally abused me for ten hours straight—and I couldn't even sleep. I just sat staring at the ceiling. It was the absolute loneliest I had ever felt in my life. And day two was the next morning.

"Day two? I can't make a day two! I will have a nervous breakdown!" I said to myself in terror. Then, I tried to think of a thousand ways to get out of it. But I couldn't. I made a commitment, and I needed the money. Whoever was in control of my universe was sure playing a cruel joke.

The next morning, with a couple hours of sleep and a few free donuts inside me, I put my whistle in my mouth and made it to center court. I tossed the jump ball. Perfectly straight. Perfect height. Then the point guard drove to the hoop and got an easy contact call. I blew my whistle hard and with authority.

"Two Shots! Line up!" I yelled at them like it was boot camp. I noticed something happening to me. After reffing ten games in a row the previous day, I was kind of getting good at it. The next game, the same thing. The abuses also simmered. By the fourth game, the tournament director came over to me.

"You are doing a pretty good job. Keep it up!"

As the day went on, my whistles were getting louder and my calls more confident. I was actually having … fun? I wouldn't need therapy after all! After the championship game, I called the tournament director over and handed him my whistle.

"Heard you also need City League refs?"

"Sure do!" he replied.

I grabbed the whistle back from his hands.

"I'll be there!" Twenty-four hours ago, I thought I fouled out of the game of life and was about to blame the referee of the universe. Instead, I got back on the court again and made a hell of a rebound.

# YES, YOU CAN!

The sins of this sixth-grade swimmer at the city pool ran deep. "No running! Keep off the Ledge! Don't splash the lifeguard! Do not intentionally plug that kid's snorkel!" I've heard them all, and they were sounding like a broken record.

Then the city hired Sid as the head lifeguard and swim coach. Sid had red hair flowing like a summer campfire. Every time he spoke, the whole pool could hear him as his deep voice echoed off the deep end. He didn't know how to whisper. Every sentence he muttered was at the decibel of a Marine drill sergeant. He walked around with an intimidating permanent scowl on his face, hovering over that barrel chest of his. The usual timid teenage lifeguard whistles became less frequent as every kid feared the wrath of a Shawshank Sid tirade if you dared to break a rule.

To make matters worse, I was on the swim team that year. Every morning, I would jump into that shriveling cold water with zero warm fuzzies from Coach Sid. Lap after lap, I would listen to Sid bark something that even penetrated the splashes of the water. I didn't even know there were that many things one could say to a swimmer. Something other than a compliment, that is, compliments were not a part of Sid's vocabulary. Lap after lap we would all swim in military-like fashion with fear being the motivating factor.

One day at swim practice, Sid offered some instruction on my swimming technique. What Sid probably said was something simple, like:

"Hey Dave, I need you to do something for me."

But what I heard in my head was something like, "LISTEN PRIVATE PYLE! YOU NO GOOD WORTHLESS, GUPPY! MY PET SWIMS BETTER THAN YOU, AND I HAVE A PET ROCK! THIS IS WAR!"

It was the first time Sid even said my name, and I didn't say a word. I was too scared because just last week he held my brother Jon's head underwater, almost drowning him until he did a flip turn. I stood there at the four-foot shallow end, looking up at him with abused puppy eyes shivering in the cold water. Sid then gave me good clear swimming instruction.

"Dave, you are turning your head right as you take your breath with every third stroke. I want you to alternate taking a breath on your right side, then on your left side with every third stroke."

It was simple instruction, but again what I heard in my head was, "YOU DON'T EVEN KNOW HOW TO BREATHE! MY GREAT GRANDMOTHER CAN BREATHE BETTER THAN YOU AND SHE'S BEEN DEAD FOR FIFTY YEARS!"

At this point, I have been swimming all my short life. And every time I did the American Crawl (They called it the American Crawl, then because perhaps the Canadian crawl looks way different when the water is ice) I would take my breaths to the right. It was my habit; all I knew; it was all I ever knew. I was not changing. Not now. Not for Sid. It would be the first time all season. In a soft, high-pitched eleven-year-old voice, I said my first words back to Sid, the monster.

"But … I can't turn my head left to breathe…"

I could barely even finish the sentence when Sid sprung like a bobcat toward a rabbit! His scary eyes were now piercing. Bent over to stare me directly in the eye. It was the most attention he had ever given me, and I didn't want it. He only said three words.

"YES, YOU CAN!"

He said it louder than I had ever heard Sid say anything before. It shook my whole being. I wanted to cry, but the whole swimming team was staring at me, wondering why in the world I would say that to him. Sid then turned around and talked to the rest of the team. I just wanted to swim again so the water would hide my tears. I do not remember what else Sid said to the team. All I remember are those three words.

"YES, YOU CAN!".

Sid then gave the orders to swim more laps. At this point, I didn't have a choice. It was swimming the way Sid told you to or die as far as I was concerned. I started my first three strokes, then turned my head to the right as usual.

"YES, YOU CAN!" the words still shaking my whole body as I began my next few strokes.

The third stroke came, and I turned my head to breathe to the left. I did it! Three strokes, then right, then three strokes to the left. I did it! I'm not going to die today! I finished my laps, but Sid said nothing (If he only knew the value of an "attaboy"). At this point, I didn't want him to, but a part of me was glowing because, amid the abuse, I did it. The motivation was fear, but I did it and I kept on doing it. For the rest of my life, if in a difficult situation, I envision him looking at me in the eye and shouting those three words.

"YES, YOU CAN!"

# LUCKY RABBIT'S FEET

It was the first time I had stepped inside a Catholic Church, and I had never been so excited to go to a church. I was actually in the church gym, where they were doing their annual Sacred Heart carnival. My eight-year-old eyes widened as I stepped through the door. I thought I was going to have a nice, calm small town Friday night, but these guys did it right. Along each wall were many games, prizes, and commotion. The little old lady at the door asked me if I wanted to buy some tickets. I gave her my total savings—about five bucks for five tickets. The place was packed and friends from around the town were all walking around with all sorts of stuffed animals, trinkets, and prizes. I bypassed the ring toss and headed for the stage where they had a table full of glorious cakes.

"How do you win a cake?" I asked in my innocent little kid voice. (For the wecord, I weely liked using sentences that didn't have any 'R's in it).

In a cheerful voice, the girl running the game said, "Oh, this is a cakewalk! It's so fun. What you do is walk around this circle with numbers on it while the music is playing. When the music stops, stand on a number. If I call out your number, you win a cake!"

That sounds easy enough, I thought as I handed over my dollar ticket. "The Winner Takes It All" by ABBA started playing and I walked around in circles. This wasn't quite as fun as the cheerful girl made it out to be. The music stopped, and I landed on number three. "Twelve!" She called out. Well, down a dollar. I gave her another ticket as I laid the roots of my adult gambling habit. This time, "All Out of Love" by Air Supply started playing as I again walked around a circle like those horses I saw at the fair. Suddenly, the music stopped, and this time I was bound to win. I was standing on lucky number seven. I looked over at the cakes and my mouth gave a Pavlov response. "Two!" the girls yelled out and just like that, I was down to just three bucks.

Disgusted at the two dollars I just wasted; I went down to find another game. One game had several fishing poles. For just one ticket, I could dangle my line over a cardboard refrigerator box decorated like an ocean. Guaranteed winner!

Every cast came back up with a prize. I happily gave them my ticket and dangled my line over the box.

"Surely, I would come up with a glorious prize."

I thought, "It was a church, after all."

I pulled my line up with anticipation. On the hook was just some ten-cent plastic ring. "I just paid a dollar for this?" Heartbroken, I just left the ring with them and now I was down to just two tickets. I really had to make these last two count, so I walked around a bit, studying the rest of the games, when another kid walked by with something that caught my eye.

"What is that!" I asked Wayne who went to Lincoln School.

Usually, I lead any conversation with a Lincoln school kid with "Lincoln, Stinkin, what you been drinkin! Could it be Whisky? Could it be wine? I think it was Turpentine!" but I needed information and decided to be nice.

"It's a lucky rabbit's foot!" Wayne answered as proudly as a dog who had just caught a rabbit. It was a real rabbit's foot but bright orange with a shade of green with a key chain on it. I wanted one, and I wanted one bad. The thought of some redneck figuring out how to market all his leftover rabbit's feet after slaughtering the rabbits never occurred to me. Nor did the thought of how it could be lucky, because it sure wasn't lucky for the rabbit.

"Where do you get one?" I asked, and he pointed to the game at the end.

"All you have to do is knock all the bottles off the tire," he said proudly.

I darted for the game and handed him my fourth ticket. On the prize table were rabbits' feet of all different colors. Man, I couldn't wait to go to school that Monday with a rabbit's foot around my belt loop.

I snatched three baseballs and took my three shots at the bottles. I could hear the Little League umpire in my head.

"BALL THREE!" as I whiffed three times.

Then, I gave my last dollar. I thought of all the Aluminum cans I collected to get those five bucks. I thought about how my hands stunk picking up all those Olympia cans.

The pressure was mounting. I threw my first ball. "Crack!" I hit it right down the ol' pipe! But my eight-year-old arm was no Nolan Ryan. Only a couple of bottles fell over. I threw the second ball, and it was a miss. I looked again over at all the rabbits' feet and thought about my stupid ten-cent ring and the stupid cakewalk. This was my last chance. It would all be worth it if I could just get a rabbit's foot.

I threw my third ball.

"Crack!" A direct hit. All the bottles fell, but one stood there wobbling.

"C'mon, fall down!" I yelled as it wobbled and wobbled but didn't fall.

Holding back the tears, I wandered outside the doors towards my Star Wars banana seat bike. Call it lucky, call it a miracle, but there on the ground lay something bright, shiny, and furry. It was a lucky rabbit's foot with a broken key chain.

I proudly wore the red and orange foot to school that Monday. Even Todd, a sixth grader, seemed impressed.

"Cool! I actually lost one just like that! I don't know where that thing went."

# BOND WITH THE WIND

"Hccckkkkkkkkkttttt ... phutttttttttt!" What I thought was going to be the greatest loogie in the Eastern hemisphere was actually the way Mongolians say "OK!". You see, a few years ago, I was lucky enough to be asked to go on an expedition to dig dinosaurs with the famed paleontologist Jack Horner, who was my professor in college. I was in the front seat of a Russian 4x4 van in the middle of the Mongolian desert and the last time I saw a road was six hours ago. Out of the corner of my eye, I saw my first herd of camels. I pointed with a "WOW!" like a New Yorker who had seen their first buffalo in Yellowstone. The Mongolian driver interpreted my "wow" as a demand to go see the camels. I didn't mean to, but we then took an immediate left to drive out of the way to look at camels. I tried to tell the driver, "Oh no, that's ok, we can keep going!" But using English to the Mongolian was futile and I think he interpreted that as "I'll give you five bucks if you drive towards the camels!"

This irritated Jack, as he was on a mission. Jack eats, drinks, and sleeps dinosaurs. Perhaps this was even a little embarrassing to him, as seeing camels in Mongolia is equivalent to seeing cows in Montana. I shrugged my shoulders at him in the back seat and cringed, saying "I didn't mean to".

I felt sheepish but secretly excited to go look at camels! After a few touristy photos, I got back in the front seat and kept my mouth shut the rest of the way. It was thirteen total hours to our destination, and we still had seven to go. Back in my hometown of Glendive, I could find a dinosaur within ten minutes of my home. But Mongolia was different. Muslims have Mecca, Jews have Jerusalem, Catholics have The Vatican, Rednecks have Walmart and paleontologists have Mongolia. All paleontologists dream of going to Mongolia.

The sun set, and we had not yet made our destination. Our plan was, whenever the sun was setting, that's where we would camp. The magic of Mongolia is that there are no fences—the land belongs to everyone. It felt so free. It's been that way for a thousand years. There were no barbed wire fences to rip my clothes on. There was no, "Keep out!" Or "No trespassing" signs. There was no "Camp in designated spaces only!" We were completely free. The feeling resonated with my soul as if it were the first day an innocent man was set free after a life in prison. I took out my tent and the feeling quickly vanished.

"Oh No!" I thought to myself. I just remembered this was a brand-new tent! That meant I had to figure out how to put up this tent in front of everyone … especially Jack, who used to spend months in the jungles of Vietnam as a marine.

I stared at that tent like Superman, staring at Kryptonite. I tried to impress a girl once by building her an IKEA desk she bought. She hasn't talked to me since, but she has a nice nightstand and some firewood. The rest of the crew stared at me, as they all had their tents up. The pressure was on. Then it clicked. "Oh, the long orange rods were backward!"

Just then, a smiling Mongolian grabbed the tent and pointed to himself. "ACCHHTTT PPTTEE CKKLXX" he said smiling.

"Oh no, that's ok. I just figured it out." I replied, but it was too late.

It was just gibberish to him. He thought he was doing me a huge favor, but having another man put up my tent in front of a Vietnam Vet was the worst thing he could do.

Jack called me "soft" and he was doubting his choice of bringing me. First the camels and now this. I was not looking too good here and all because of this darn language barrier.

The next day we made our destination. The terrain looked just like Makoshika Park, only upside down. My job, along with my new friend Matt and three Mongolians, was to chisel out a poor family of one-hundred-million-year-old complete psittacosaurus (a small dinosaur with a parrot beak) stuck in sandstone that had cemented. It was tedious work.

My goal that week was to work as hard as the Mongolians. I wasn't even close. They were all amazing, and it was easy to see how Genghis Khan ruled the world. Still, it was awkward working next to them all day without being able to communicate.

The first day, we all pounded away without saying a word to each other. Then, the next day, a breakthrough happened. I'll blame it on the amazing Mongolian cooking, but as men do, I may have perhaps broken wind a little bit … ok maybe it was quite a bit. I gave the same sheepish look earlier with the camels and my tent struggles.

They all stopped their work for the first time and laughed at me. "Wind!"

One Mongolian knew only a few words and "wind" was one of them.

"Wind!" I replied, laughing.

Soon, all five of us were laughing. I smiled the rest of the day as I contemplated my surreal situation, chiseling away at one-hundred-million-year-old dinosaurs on the other side of the world with my new friends, who only had one word in common. "Wind".

Yes, "wind"! This must be the secret to world peace!

Dear Mr. President, I think if you gave me just thirty seconds at the beginning of the next world summit meeting, I believe I will bring world peace.

Make sure the meeting is after dinner, of course!

# OLYMPIC DREAMS

As I watched the beer-bellied curling winner of the 2018 Winter Olympics step on the podium, I had an epiphany. Thanks to bowling and curling, my childhood dreams of either becoming a professional or Olympic athlete were still alive! Curling especially intrigued me. I had no idea what was going on as they slid those stones across the ice, but I knew with all that sweeping going on, I would have a distinct advantage over any young millennial. The Rocky theme song played in my head. Gold Medal visions danced in my head. Perhaps my hometown would throw me a parade or even a statue. I could display that gold medal on my fridge next to my 2nd place brownies ribbon from the county fair of 2014. Ahh … yes, the golden adulation deepened my daydream.

I called my buddy Russ, "Hey, I want to go curling!"

By coincidence, he replied, "I just visited my sister in Missoula, and I went curling for the first time a few weeks ago. It was awesome! I also started an Olympic team."

"Wow," I thought, this must be destiny. "I'm in! When do we start to train?"

Russ answered, "Well, you have to try out for my team first."

Just one paragraph before this, I actually called Russ my buddy.

"You have to beat me. If you beat me, then you are on the team."

Well, he was the one with all this curling experience. I guess fair is fair. We then looked for a place to go curling.

If only we could go to Canada. But Canada is another country, so it must be incredibly far away.

Out of curiosity, we asked Alexa, "Alexa, how far away is Canada?"

Alexa replied, "I'm sorry, I don't know the answer."

I tried again, "Alexa, how far is Canada … Eh?"

She then promptly replied, "One hundred and fifty miles to the border."

"What? Russ, did you know Canada was so close? Why doesn't anybody ever go there? Let's go curling!"

Russ agreed, and we made plans for an upcoming weekend.

We arrived at the border and the guard asked what we were going to do in Canada.

I was honest. "Curling!!"

The guard replied with a look sterner than a curling stone.

"Pull over, please."

I think my answer was a first for him. The border was actually very easy, and we were on our way. We made no previous arrangements. All we had was an address to a curling center in Regina and we thought we would just show up and hope for the best.

Russ and I found the curling center and walked in like two kids in a candy store. We told the fellow at the counter we traveled from Montana just to go curling, not knowing what to expect. He couldn't have been nicer.

"Oh, yoo bet! Have at er! The league comes in aboot an hour or soo, so just help yerselves until then!"

He wouldn't even take our money. It turned out that every Canadian we met on that trip was just as nice. I got the impression that Canada and the U.S. are like my middle school playground and the Canadians were the sixth graders. The sixth graders were the nice kids who didn't dare go to the eighth-grade side of the playground, because eighth-graders are unpredictable, even though they shared the same playground.

Russ and I put on the special curling shoes and headed to the ice. I only fell twice. I grabbed the first stone as we both did a couple of practice runs. Of course, I was a bit nervous. This was my first Olympic tryout after all, and I really wanted this.

I remembered watching the Olympics and tried to emulate their style as best as I could—observing how much they stretched and I tried to do the same. I pulled a groin. True story. That didn't stop me, though. Russ was going down, and I was going to make his Olympic team. The score was back and forth. It was just us two, so we didn't have sweepers. We didn't need them, anyway; we were Americans.

As fate would have it, the score came down to the last stone thrown. It was all up to me. If I scored with my stone, then fame, fortune, glory and the adulation of every woman would all be mine. Like a champion, I blocked out my pulled groin and gave that stone a gentle curl.

The slow anticipation of the slide across the ice was almost more than I could bear. It looked like a good line. My pulse beat faster and my heart jumped into my throat. My groin did too. The stone eased closer to the middle. All I had to do was beat Russ's last throw and I'm on the team. Could it be? The stone slowed to a finish just short, and the mighty Casey had struck out.

Destiny denied. My "buddy" Russ started laughing at me.

"I guess you're not on the team. Try back in four more years."

"Hey Russ," I took my defeat like a man, "Do you think we could look for a bowling ball while we are here? I think it's cheaper in Canada."

# A CALIFORNIA CHRISTMAS

It was NOT the best of times; it was the worst of times. I felt like an evergreen among a patch of palm trees. After one fine glorious Glendive day of fishing, swimming, baseball, or whatever daily adventure in this personal Disneyland I grew up in, I walked into the house and my parents broke the news out of the blue to my stunned pubescent face.

"We are moving to San Diego, California!"

The news hit me like a crashing wave. Like many Californians before, my parents moved there searching for gold. The oil around Glendive was drying up. They had to do something. But unfortunately, the gold in California, at least for us, was hiding under rainbows.

It was my first move, and I could tell you sad stories of trying to make friends, strange schools and blah, blah, blah, but worst of all was Christmas.

Nothing felt more wrong than a 72.5-degree California Christmas. You will never see a Hallmark Christmas movie about a Californian. They do not even have chimneys for Santa to go down. Those kids must have been so confused. Nobody looks like Santa in California, everyone is skinny. Do Californian Kindergartners even leave Santa cookies? I bet they leave avocados and tofu. They have no fireplaces to roast chestnuts. (Ok, I have never roasted chestnuts either, but I jumped over a bonfire in college once on a dare.) There are no silver bells, no Christmas trees, and except for a few confiscations along the border, no white Christmas either.

Do these kids even know the joy of putting on seven layers of clothing and a pair of Moon Boots? All the while having their snot frozen to a ski mask as their sled clears enough air to add another color bruise on the butt bone. No, instead they must go surfing. Ok, I'll call that one a tie, but still; nothing feels less like Christmas than a California Christmas.

The band Everclear once stated in a lyric, "I hate those people who love to tell you money is the root of all that kills. They have never had the joy of a welfare Christmas."

Our family wasn't on welfare, but we also didn't have a Nintendo. I think in 1987, that was a question on your income tax. "Do you have kids sixteen and under who do not have a Nintendo? Check yes or no." When my brothers and I would go to the mall, we would stop, head right to the electronics, and stare at the Nintendo for sale as if we were Gollum in Lord of the Rings.

"My precious! My precious!"

It was torture. I would have done anything to get my hands on a Nintendo.

Dad went through the ebbs and flows of different jobs, like the Pacific tides. Nothing ever seemed to work out. It was just one imaginary pot of gold after another. We were coming upon our second California Christmas and neither I nor my brothers dared to ask for anything.

Socks and underwear at this point would have been as good as my Star Wars Millennium Falcon back when I was eight.

Dad came home one day with a smile on his face. "I got a job running a Christmas Tree lot this year! It is even going to have live reindeer! But I am going to need your help."

70

At this point, life couldn't surprise me anymore. Consistency would have been the surprise. "Christmas Trees? Reindeer?" This one surprised even me.

Dad was also the master at exaggerating and putting a positive spin on things, but he was right on with this one. His new job was to manage a Christmas tree lot of all things. And they even had caged reindeer. It was a bit 'Barnum and Bailey'. They advertised "COME SEE SANTA'S REINDEER" but they were really a species of regular deer they said was 'rescued'. Didn't matter to me, I named one Randolph. Randolph was Rudolph's twin brother, whose butt lit up instead of his nose. Poor guy kept blinding Santa and got kicked off the team (This also may explain my lack of friend-making ability).

The bad news was Dad couldn't afford to pay us much, and the days were long. Still, working with Christmas trees all day had a certain charm and smell to it. I didn't mind.

Opening day came, and it was busy. We had the biggest tree lot in San Diego, and it turns out, Californians were desperate for some kind of real Christmas in their life. They couldn't get snow, but they could get a tree. I helped the first customer bring the tree to their car, and she gave me a few dollars! Didn't expect a tip; I didn't know I'd get a tip, but everyone tipped me for bringing their tree to the car. Suddenly, I got visions of Super Mario Brothers.

"My Precious!"

Two weeks of this and I could finally afford a Nintendo. In a good mood, I started singing like Julie Andrews. "Barefoot on beaches and middle fingers for no blinker. Smog-colored clouds and my lungs were less pink. Brown paper packages cops got from a sting. These are a few of my favorite things."

California was growing on me. I hauled tree after tree. The tips piled up just in time for Christmas. My brothers and I all pitched in and entered the higher tax bracket. We now owned a Nintendo!

We must have played for seventy-two hours straight until our hands literally didn't work anymore, then slept on the beanbag in front of the TV while the other brother played. For seventy-two hours straight, we didn't care what state we were in. We didn't care about what job was next after the Christmas trees. We didn't care that we had another snowless Christmas. Everything was just fine living in Super Mario World.

# THIS CREEK IS MY CREEK, THIS CREEK IS YOUR CREEK

The big Montana sky was as blue as could be. The summertime birds were singing. A light breeze cooled the back of my suntanned neck. Even at ten years old, I've watched enough Disney movies to know this must be what it would feel like to live in a Disney movie on this fine small-town summer day.

A beat-up fishing pole on my back and a can of worms in my pocket from the thunderstorm the night before. I headed to my usual favorite fishing spot past the Little League field in such a good mood; I sang the new song we learned in school this year. "This land is your land ... this land is my land ... from California ... to the New York Island, this land was made for you and me!"

As I kept humming the tune, I did something different that day. "It's time to try a new spot today," I thought.

I moved upstream a bit. I was always in search of Omar Moreno. That's the name I gave to the eight-pound catfish that snapped my line the year before. I vowed revenge.

"From the Redwood Forest ... to the Gulf Stream waters..."

I kept singing as I wandered past the football field and stepped into a wooded forest near the river. Within a few steps, I heard a yelling from a house on the hill.

"Hey! Hey kid! You can't go there. That is private property!"

"But … but … this land is my land?" I mumbled to myself as I stood a bit scared stiff from being yelled at. It looked like the same land as my favorite fishing spot, but the man kept yelling at me to get off his property.

The sky was not as blue as it had once been, and the credits started rolling in my Disney movie. I turned around with my head down and went home. I wasn't in the mood to fish anymore.

I came back a couple of days later with my childhood friend, Cody. He didn't believe me.

"I'm telling you, if you step two feet off the football field, that guy will start yelling at you."

He had to see it for himself. I stayed back, but Cody ventured in.

"Hey! Hey!" It was like clockwork. "You can't go there. That's private property!"

Cody gave me a baffled look, then we ran away. A couple of weeks later Cody and I went fishing again, this time with another friend unfamiliar with our fishing grounds.

Cody whispered to me, "Hey Dave, watch this."

Cody then gave orders to Brian. "Hey, Brian…the best hole is just past the football field. You can have that one. We'll give it to you for being new."

Brian thanked us and took off for the good hole past the football field while Cody and I tried to keep our laughter in. Sure enough, within thirty seconds of stepping past the football field boundary…

"Hey! Hey Kid! This is private property!"

Cody and I burst out laughing as poor Brian took his verbal beating from the man standing on the hill.

Last summer, in late August, I was kayaking down my beloved Yellowstone River. I pulled over in a large tributary creek and waded up the creek looking for turtles. I was filming "Life on the Yellowstone" for my YouTube channel and needed some good animal footage. Having quite a bit of Walter Mitty in me as I waded up that creek, in my head, I imagined I was hired by National Geographic to do their next amazing Glendive Montana story. Suddenly, I unexpectedly saw a man up and around the bend.

"Ahh…a fellow Montanan. Montanans are always friendly. I'll have myself a good chat," I thought to myself.

I waved at him with a smile. When I got his attention, he started yelling at me.

"Hey! Hey! The river is that way!" and gave a condescending point towards the river.

Maybe it was from some Freudian childhood thing, but I hate getting yelled at, especially condescending like that. We shouted a few more words as I pleaded my case that I was legal and only taking pictures, but he was having none of it.

"This is private property!" He yelled over, "Even the creek!"

I decided it wasn't worth it. So, I walked back to the kayak and fished for a bit.

While fishing downstream, I noticed the man was now at the river, but just a football field away from me.

"Well, I'm going to talk to him face to face and get to the bottom of this. I want to make sure I am legal."

I paddled a hundred yards towards him, and he had a curious look on his face as I drew nearer. In my most calm diplomatic un-confrontational voice, I struck up a conversation asking exactly where he thought his property line was. Who was right or wrong is another story, but our conversation ended up being the nice Montana conversation it ought to be.

After a long ten-minute conversation about our shared love of the Yellowstone, I finally asked his name. Once he told me his name, I laughed as hard as Cody and I did when we sent poor unsuspecting Brian over.

"What's so funny?" He asked, bewildered. I replied, "Forty years ago, your dad used to chase me off HIS land, too!!"

# THE BROTHER BOWL

I've always been thankful we have a holiday where it's appropriate to give your family the bird. The traditions of Thanksgiving run deep with words of the sixth letter in the Alphabet. Family, friends, feasts, and foremost football! If those early pilgrims had shot a pig instead of a turkey, we could have killed two birds with one stone (or should I say saved two birds) by instead eating ham and throwing around the ole pigskin it came from. Growing up Glendive, football with friends on the Friday after T-day had become as much a tradition in my mind as putting olives on all my fingers before I eat them. Throughout grade school, The Friday football game was the best part of Thanksgiving break and even in college, the neighborhood friends would still get together for a pickup game.

One particular year, all my four brothers were in town. I called a few friends and the ones that showed up; I realized it was looking like a high school alumnus all-star team. Some were on-track scholarships, and some held track school records that still exist today. It was going to be some tough football, but I wasn't too worried. All I had to do was guard one of my brothers and I could keep up. They would say the same about me.

"Ok, what's the teams?" I asked. If we were going to pick teams, I knew they'd pick me at about the same time as Mom's cranberry Jello salad on my plate. Last!

"How about all the brothers as a team?" One of the alumnus all-stars quipped. I think he was joking, and if he wasn't, it was still a funny comment.

But before I could say "That's a worse idea than pie without cool whip," my older competitive brother Hunter shouted, "It's on!"

We elected to receive the ball first.

"Alright," Hunter said as he took the ball, designating himself quarterback. "This is how we are going to do this."

He began drawing up football plays never seen before.

"This first play, I need you to all huddle around me with your backs towards me. One of you is going to get the ball tucked behind your shirt. When they count to five Mississippi, we all disperse like feathers on a turkey. They won't know who has the ball."

Hunter then gave the proverbial "Hut!" and as the rush came, none of the all-stars had seen anything like it as we all went in different directions. They were too confused to tackle anyone.

Touchdown!

Now the all-stars were a bit agitated and promptly scored. It was our turn and again, Hunter drew up another play in the huddle.

"This time, Dave, I need you to limp. Complain about your ankle the whole way to the line. When I say HUT, keep limping for a second. When your defender sees you're hurt, he'll back off. As soon as he does, take off running as fast as you can. I'll get you the ball!"

I did my best Hollywood back to the line of scrimmage and sure enough, the defender backed off and I took off running.

Another Touchdown!

On the next possession, we designed another play. We all got on one side of the field. Hunter lateralled the football to one brother, who quickly lateralled it to another brother and then another and then another like we were a clown act putting out a fire at a circus.

Finally, while still behind the line of scrimmage, making it legal, the last brother then threw it back to Hunter, whom the all-stars had completely forgotten about by this point.

Another touchdown!

By this time, the all-stars were completely bewildered. Hunter drew up more plays on the spot.

"Ok, this time I am going to act like I am going to throw the ball, but Dave, you come from behind and take the ball. Then, stuff the ball behind my shirt as you take it, but keep running. They will follow you and think you have the ball, and I'll take off running."

Another touchdown!

The all-stars eventually threw the white flag like they were on their third helping of stuffing. They just couldn't take anymore. It was like defending David Copperfield or clowns in a clown car. On that historical day, I saw what the power of family can do. Individually, we were outmatched. They were turkey; we were mashed potatoes. But it is the complete meal that makes Thanksgiving, not just the turkey. By working together, the sum became greater than its parts. I realized then that it is the whole meal that makes a family, not just a couple of pieces of turkey.

# THE GREAT PRANK OF 2020

"I would like a Big Mac, please." My college roommate and friend Chris said as he ordered with a southern charm in his voice. I was already at the table with my McNuggets. Chris had movie star good looks, extreme confidence, and charisma. In fact, he later would model and act for a short time in the soap opera "Guiding Light". I was merely an Ed McMahon to his Johnny Carson, the Robin to his Batman, or the Tattoo to his Fantasy Island. Chris leaned in closer to the girl working the McDonald's restaurant register.

"I have to tell you, that's my friend Dave who just ordered before me and he's incredibly shy, but he has a HUGE crush on you!"

The girl working the register blushed with a grimace. Chris then sat down as I had a mouthful of fries, oblivious to his conversation with the McCashier girl.

"Oh, hey ... I forgot to order fries," Chris said. "Could you order some for me? I'm starving!"

Being the people pleaser that I am, I was happy to do so as Chris handed me a couple of dollars. I came back with the fries and exclaimed, "Dude! Did you see how the girl at the register was looking at me?" I arrogantly said to Chris being the first time I got the attention instead of him.

"Why are you laughing? What's so funny!?"

"Oh…nothing", Chris replied behind a snicker. "Nothing at all." As he said with another sly laugh.

This was the daily life of being a sidekick. The entertainment value of hanging with Chris outweighed the daily embarrassment.

The next week Chris and I were studying in the library (Yes, studying. True story, I swear). It was early in the semester and two new attractive girls we didn't know walked in and sat a couple tables away. I turned to nudge Chris, but he was instinctively gone.

"Uh oh", I thought. I felt like I had just entered a haunted house. I didn't know what, or how, but I knew something was going to get me.

Just then, Chris made the loudest manufactured noise of passing gas from behind a bookcase. It was one of his talents and the noise was spot on. Both girls stared at me, horrified. I thought the situation was so funny; I burst into laughter, which made me look even guiltier. Just another day of being a Chris sidekick.

Later that year, I noticed my hair getting blonder and blonder. A bit perplexed on why, but for some reason, I was proud of this. I felt like my inner surfer looks from my California high school years were coming back. It was a bit strange for this to happen in the middle of a Montana winter. Even so, I was proud of my "natural" new surfer looks. I remember Jason, the center of the basketball team, coming up to me.

"Did you dye your hair, Dave?"

Proudly, I replied, "No way, all-natural man!".

He prodded some more with a snicker each time. I realized later he had some information from Chris that I had not figured out yet. Chris, my roommate, put "Sun-in" (a product that turns hair blonde with sunlight) into my shampoo. I didn't even figure it out until a year later.

Officer Osborn was the local police officer who often gave the eighteen-year-olds of Glendive (perhaps deserved) a tough time. Ever the actor, Chris had a spot-on imitation of Officer Osborn. To tell this next story would take another thousand words, so I will just give you four. Forgive the foils of my youth, but it involved such words as Halloween, eggs, cops, and escaping.

Later that night, I got a call at 2:00 AM from Officer Osborn. He said the police were coming over to take me in. At that same time, Chris hung up the phone at another house and said, "He fell for it hook, line, and sinker!" to the rest of my circle of friends, who all started howling with laughter.

I fell for it so hard that when my friends came knocking on my door to reveal the prank; they found me on the phone with my brother getting law advice—at two in the morning.

Today, Chris is still one of my best friends. He still pulls pranks on me with the last one just a few years ago. Chris filmed me talking about dinosaurs, then posted the video online without me knowing after "Hollywooding" the video up a bit. The Dinodave video went mini-viral, so we kept doing more videos, but now it's on purpose.

I reminisce and relish those days when my biggest worry was how I was going to get pranked. I think and wish those days were now. That perhaps if only 2020 was a grand, giant prank. I mean, who would have thought a tiny RNA strand with the size of .0000008 of an inch could stop the world in its tracks? It would be the prank of the century! Nobody would see it coming or know what to do. If only Chris and my college friends would come crashing through the door at any moment, rip off their masks, and start laughing.

"We got you! Oh man, we got you hook, line, and sinker!" If only 2020 could be known as the greatest prank of all time. It sure feels that way.

# UP THE CREEK WITHOUT A PADDLEFISH

You are not a true Glendivian unless you have done this or that is a perfect subject for a future book. A few years ago, I needed to put a checkmark next to paddle fishing. For those who fly first class and have never had the joy of feeling like a middle-seat ham sandwich between a couple of three-hundred-pound buns on their way back from sweaty Las Vegas, let me explain:

You see … I had just moved back from Bozeman Mountain. Every time I walked into a snooty western Montana fly shop; I would get the same feeling I would get by walking past first class to the end of the plane. Those nobles who sat reclined, sunglasses on, drinking their free drink with one pinky finger in the air (and another specific finger in the air with their thoughts).

You would never get that attitude when paddle fishing (a prehistoric plankton-eating fish that weighed more than Delta would ever allow and could only be snagged with a large treble hook) and it was something I had to try.

The limit for paddlefish is just one per person and my brother had just caught him. He lent me his ten-foot pole and tackle as I made my way down the local Intake diversion dam that causes the paddlefish to congregate as they have trouble swimming past.

The paddle fishing at Intake can get crowded, and on this day, there were at least thirty fishermen. I know this because every fifth t-shirt was a Duck Dynasty shirt, and I counted six.

A little nervous and intimidated, a spot opened, and I stepped in sheepishly. The guy to the left of me had a beard that probably grew downward in direct proportion to his belly outward. He had an old spark plug for a weight because ninety-nine cents was too much to buy one from the store.

His pole was bigger than mine, too, and I almost stepped away. I couldn't fish next to a guy with a bigger pole, and I already lacked confidence. I watched him cast first and the dang thing went halfway across the river. Man, this guy was confident. I went for my first cast, and I looked just like Rob Gronkowski spiking a football after a touchdown, as my hook didn't even make the water. I just knew what the guy next to me was thinking:

"I bet this guy can't even change a tire."

He was right.

Then the guy to the right of me went for a cast, not to be outdone by the guy with the long pole. Another cast to the middle of the river. These guys were really trying to outdo each other. The pressure was on as I attempted my second cast ever. At this point, it no longer became important to catch a paddlefish, it was more important to show a respectable cast.

I flipped the bale and wound my pole back. Again, I mistimed my throw, and my hook and sinker went just further than a Canadian first down. On a scale of one to ten, I'd rate this cast as a 'Rosie O'Donnell'.

Embarrassed, I gave a quick pull and acted like I meant to cast there even though there would never be a paddlefish that close to shore. My line was now only ten feet away from shore and gave a second tug, hoping to snag something. Suddenly, the Pavlov sound of my drag kicked in, the tension of my line straightened, and my ten-foot pole was now a curve.

"Fish on!"

The Larry the Cable Guy target audience that surrounded me looked in awe as they had been casting for hours. Surely it must be a snag, but it was no snag. On my second pull of my second cast, ten feet from shore, I had hooked into my first paddlefish.

The line of fishermen along the shore reeled in politely as I began my fight to redeem my manhood. They all wanted to see what the dumbest fish in Yellowstone looked like as badly as I did. It didn't take long to reel in. After all, I hooked into it only ten feet away.

As my brother pulled the forty-five-pound paddlefish to shore, he yelled, "Hey, where's the paddle?"

"What do you mean, where's the paddle? It's literally called a paddlefish." I shot back.

"Well, you just caught a fish then, because this paddlefish has no paddle."

I set the pole down and ran over as he brought it to shore. It was true, I had caught a paddlefish without a paddle. It was literally gone. My fish just had a stub in front of his nose instead of a paddle.

For over sixty-five million years, the paddlefish have been around, and for sixty-five million years, they have all had paddles. All but this one.

"These things happen to me," I thought to myself as the crowd snickered to themselves. Maybe that's why I caught her so close to shore. She was probably picked on her whole life and was barred from swimming with the rest of the paddlefish. They would say things like

"Hey, don't go up any creeks without a paddle!" or "Hey carp face, what are you doing tonight?" or, "Am I just being nosey?"

I felt bad for her and if it wasn't the law that I had to keep her, I would have released the poor girl.

Alas, I was proud to catch the only paddleless paddlefish in the Yellowstone River. I took a proud picture with me and Miss Stubnose as I forever laid down that ten-foot pole with a smile that may as well have said, "Mr. Dave, we are going to bump you into first class."

# THE TROUBLE WITH CURVES

Just as I shoveled another piece of pineapple from the Maui hotel breakfast buffet, the corner of my eye caught my friend Dave coming at me like a North Shore wave. He had that look in his eye, that "we may die today" look in his eye. I've seen it a hundred times, and that is exactly why he has been my best friend since kindergarten.

I set my pineapple down in anticipation. "Hey, I know exactly what we are going to do today!" Dave said as he sat down.

"We are driving the Hana highway!"

"The Hana who-way?" I replied, "I've never heard of it. Count me in!"

I've learned not to question Dave when he has the "We may die today" look in his eye. My usual protocol is to caffeinate my guardian angels and tell them, "Hey, today is going to be a fun day, but you're gonna have to stay on your toes". Then they give me that look that I've become so good at ignoring.

We had zero agenda. We usually never do. Plans ruin any adventure. We just took off in the rental car for whatever came our way. Dave educated me on what he read about the Hana Highway. This highway had sixty-four miles of the curviest roads you will ever see. There were actual speed limit signs that said fifteen miles per hour. We couldn't even speed if we wanted to, because it was so curved. Every few miles, there would be a one-lane bridge over a cascade. And they called this a highway? I was riding shotgun and literally getting carsick. Ever since I rode the tilt-a-whirl in sixth grade ten times in a row for free with my sister, because the greasy carney guy had a crush on my sister, I've had a tough time with motion sickness. Anyway, I told Dave. "We have to pull over, man, or I won't make it." Luckily, the next pullout was an actual coconut stand. I have a few rules I live by in life. One of them is if I pull over at a coconut stand in Hawaii, I am absolutely going to buy a coconut.

The lady at the stand had a large machete in her hand. She asked, "Do you want to machete your own coconut?" My eyes lit up because saying yes to people who ask me if I want to machete a coconut is the other rule I live by.

"Absolutely!" My voice cut with enthusiasm.

I grabbed the machete and raised it high above like a public executioner, as if this coconut spoke evil against my 12th-century king. Just as I was about to come down on this coconut like a guillotine, the coconut lady's phone rang and she told me to wait as I stood there like a six-year-old who lost his balloon. That lady was a talker and I couldn't take it anymore and yelled, "Hey Lady! I'm ready to machete!"

She thought "ready to machete" was the funniest thing and gave me the thumbs up as I gave the coconut its sentence.

The rest of the day did not disappoint. We jumped off forty-foot waterfalls with the locals; Visited amazing black sand beaches; Hiked through jungles; and packed as much adventure into one day as possible.

The sun set, but the day was not over. We still had to travel hours of the hectic Hana highway back to the hotel in the darkness of the night.

I was driving now and doing my best Andretti imitation. Dave was used to my driving and has learned to stay calm. He's on a first-name basis with all my guardian angels. At least I thought I was driving fast when a small Toyota truck with the back loaded with four of the largest Tapioca, Big Kahuna dudes I had ever seen, zipped past us. It was the only vehicle we had seen in the last hour.

Then, only five miles later, we see that truck pulled over.

"We have to stop, right, Dave?"

He agreed, it's the rules. We nervously pulled in behind them.

"Need any help?" I asked.

I felt like I just auditioned for a B horror movie.

The driver told us, "Yeah, we have a flat tire but no tire iron. Do you have a tire iron?"

A tire iron, I thought. Oh man, I definitely have seen this movie before.

"Uh … yeah, it's a rental … we probably have a tire iron."

I looked at Dave and gave a nervous shrug.

"Cool, I'll go get it," he said as his enormous cumoniwannakillyou stature walked by between us. We hadn't seen another car in the last hour. The night was so dark. These guys could really make sure Dave and I were never seen again if they wanted to.

He helped himself to the trunk as both Dave and I stood cautiously. The big Kahuna found the tire iron, then started walking towards both Dave and me slowly. The tire iron in the hand of this behemoth made an interesting silhouette against the headlights. Dave and I had escape routes planned in our heads with both eyes fixated on the tire iron. He moved closer. We stood still. He was only a step away. I held my breath.

"Keep walking … oh please keep walking…" Then, sure enough, he walked past us with the tire iron as Dave and I both let out a collective sigh. We just went from victims to heroes.

They fixed the flat tire thanks to our tire iron, and we were on our way. We made it back to civilization when suddenly there was a mile-long traffic jam! We were so tired at that point and just wanted to be home. Suddenly a "Honk!" behind us. It was our flat tire Toyota Big Kahuna friends!

"Follow us!" they yelled.

It was just like the fable of the thorn in the lion's paw. They took us through every back road that only a local would know. We bypassed the traffic jam and made it to the hotel in no time. I didn't see that coming. Wow! That Hana Highway is just full of curves!

# THE SEVEN SISTERS

"Hello, this is Dave," I answered in an irritated tone. If my phone had shown it was one of my contacts, the tone of my voice would have resembled a dog wagging its tail when its owner came home, but I expected a robot on the other line of the unknown number to sell me a warranty. To my surprise, a wise voice with the tone my grandmother would use when giving me valuable advice asked me a question.

"Have you ever heard of the Seven Sisters?"

Not wanting to sound too ignorant, I replied, "I believe so, but refresh my memory."

The lady paused for a bit, then said, "They are seven caves in a row, right in Makoshika."

Boy, was I way off. "No, I haven't heard about those seven sisters. Tell me more."

Mrs. Knapp, a long-time Glendive resident, told me in her best storyteller voice that there were caves in Makoshika, called the Seven Sisters, and that I needed to find them. This intrigued me. I've seen this movie before. Either I find some type of treasure, or I suffer an apocalyptic death. There could not be an in between and either way, count me in! Only she didn't know where they were. Mrs. Knapp had only heard of them.

"Archie is who you need to talk to. Talk to Archie Gehnert … and He will talk to you about the Seven Sisters." She let out a coy laugh and then hung up.

That out-of-the-blue phone call harrowed my mind the rest of the day. I have such an appetite for adventure, and Mrs. Knapp just gave me a taste, and now I was drooling. I quickly got Archie's information, skipped the phone call and decided to just knock on his door the old-fashioned way. An elderly man with a warm disposition and smile answered the door.

"Hi, are you Archie? My name is Dr. Indiana Jones." Well, at least in my mind that is what I said, but I told him my name was Dave Fuqua.

Fuqua does not roll off the tongue anywhere near Jones does, but in this case, it worked because he said with a smile, "Oh yes! I knew your mother in school!"

He welcomed me into his home, and I asked about the legend of the Seven Sisters. "Of course," he said, "I can tell you about the Seven Sisters."

My eyes widened, and I was captivated. Archie leaned back in his recliner and told me the story of the Seven Sisters, as if he'd been expecting all along for me to knock on his door that day. We both talked about how much both Makoshika and the Yellowstone River influenced our lives. I told him how miserable I was the last time I visited Disneyland. Long lines, overcrowding, and high prices. Give me Makoshika and the Yellowstone River over Disneyland any day. They actually have a place in Disneyland called Adventureland. Waiting in line for two hours to ride a teacup is not my idea of an adventure.

I sat and listened to Archies' childhood stories. Like how his German Shepherd saved his life when he grabbed the dog's leash while dangling off a cliff. Or his Navy Stories, about how the artillery guns were made to shatter first as the planes flew into them, and of course his stories about the Seven Sisters caves. I sat, listened, and thought about how I could teach Disney a thing or two about adventure.

Happy to receive my next clue on the mystery of the Seven Sisters, I left Archie's house and couldn't wait any longer. I headed straight for the hills. I headed in the direction I was told, and sure enough, several drainages formed several caves. The badlands are made up of dried mud from ancient river systems. I'm sure the caves have naturally changed with erosion since Archie visited them in his day, but one cave stood out from the rest. I crept up along the caked mud that was not too sturdy to get a better look. Jack London said, "The key ingredient to fear is the unknown". Caves have always been creepy to me in that way. I never know what is in them. This cave I was about to enter was definitely an unknown, but I was on an adventure, and the key ingredient for adventure is also the unknown.

I did my best to spelunker down the gumbo, and the cave was pretty magnificent. It was a dark vaulted cathedral that looked like a Catholic vampire built it. I crept a little closer into the dark. With each shade darker, my heart pounded faster.

"What are the odds of this ending well?" I thought to myself.

It was so quiet as I crept a little further into the cave, the way I used to see Shaggy do in the Scooby-Doo cartoons. I just needed to peek around this corner, then I could get out of there. I inched around the corner more when "AHHH!" I screamed like a little girl! Some creature made a lot of noise and came right at me.

"Seriously?" I said out loud to myself as I recovered.

"All that for a pigeon!"

My adventure of the Seven Sisters ended anticlimactic with … a pigeon. Disappointed, I left the cave and wondered if I had found treasure after all. After my visits with Mrs. Knapp and Archie, I realized that perhaps life treasure is not found at the end of the adventure—but during.

# THIS IS HOW YOU GLENDIVE

I've dug dinosaurs in Mongolia, hiked to the top of Machu Picchu, dived with sharks in the Galapagos, rode elephants in Thailand, and won eight dollars playing pachinko in Japan. I live for adventure. Therefore, especially during June, July, and August, I refused to leave the adventure capital of the world: Glendive, Montana.

However, not all Glendivians believe this. These are the people with nice-looking lawns.

Last Sunday, around noon, I could have also worked on my lawn. There was a better chance of me plucking my chest hairs one by one and back in 2006, I won the Carnival Cruise hairy chest competition.

Anyway, I sent my brother a text. *Any boat rides going on today?*

He must have contemplated yard work too, because he texted back instantly. *Meet me at the dock in 15 minutes!*

My brother can unload his boat faster than you can say Yellowstone River. Soon we jetted to his secret spot. A wooded island covered by a few feet of water from the spring runoff.

He turned his engine off and we then propelled ourselves through the light hum of the trolling motor. Instantly, as we snuck inside the wooded trees, it felt like we entered a portal to another world. The hum of the motor was only a diminishing minor note amongst a symphony of various avian Magnus opuses. In the shallower water, you'd hear an adrenaline splash of large carp spawning. My brother quietly drifted closer. He didn't tell me his plan. I thought we were just listening to the peaceful sound of birds when he reached for his bow, which had somehow gone unnoticed by me. Then, with the grace of a lion ready to pounce on a gazelle, he stood up, drew back his bow, and loaded an arrow with a string attached to it.

An animal-loving angel who looked like Steve Irwin appeared on my left shoulder. "Crikey, I hope he doesn't hurt the lil fella!", then on my right shoulder, an angel who looked like Ted Nugent appeared and yelled "Wang Dang Sweet Pontoon!" or something like that.

My brother let go of the drawstring and the arrow zipped into the water faster than my fork in a jar of pickles.

Bullseye!

The arrow pierced the largest carp I had ever seen! In fact, it wasn't a carp, but a bigger, similar species, the rarer buffalo fish! I heard a "Yahoo!" and a guitar solo from Nugent.

My brother turned to me. "That is how you Glendive!"

To his credit, my brother eats what he kills. He invited me to eat it with him that night.

"No Thanks," I replied. I know a carp is only a cousin of a goldfish. I'll leave the goldfish eating to my brother and drunk fraternity brothers.

Next, we boated to a nearby creek. Once again, we put the trolling motor in and quietly drifted in. Within minutes, we saw a creature so ugly that it would make your mother-in-law look like pre-Botox Pamela Anderson. An enormous alligator snapping turtle! What a rare sight! Then we saw another … and then another … and then another! I have never seen four snapping turtles in my life on the Yellowstone and here we saw four in five minutes.

My brother couldn't take it anymore. "I'm going to catch it." He slipped into the water and caught the ugly monster from behind! My brother looked at me and yelled, "That is how you Glendive!"

"Turtle soup, yahoo!" Nugent yelled as he played another guitar solo. But the music suddenly stopped as my brother let the turtle go. Irwin cracked an Australian smile as he stood there with an unplugged guitar cord in his hand.

It was an incredible day on the river. I felt like I was on a jungle tour at Disneyland. Wait, no, it wasn't. That's a lie. Disneyland is full of hour-long lines, immense crowds, expensive food, and crying kids. I think it's the most miserable place on earth. Their jungle tour is fake. Today was all real, wondrous—with no crowds! This must be the happiest place on earth.

We decided it was time to get back to our unkept lawns, and we jetted to the dock. As we were ready to load, another boat pulled into the dock.

"Well, that just cost us twenty minutes." My brother said.

He was there first. It was his right to unload his boat before we could get ours loaded. Well, so much for no crowds and no lines, I thought. But just then, the fella in the truck rolled down his window.

"You boys go ahead and get loaded!"

What? Did I hear that right? It was clearly his right of way. Who does that in this day and age? That was sure a nice thing for him to do. I then glanced at the number '16' on his Montana license plate, which signified he was from my favorite town.

Oh, that's right! "That is how you Glendive!"

# THE MIRACLE ON I-90

There are two kinds of people in this world. Those that can put in a car stereo and those that can't. In college, I drove a Chevy Astro conversion van for two main reasons. One, a VW bus would be no good because it could only top out at seventy-five miles per hour, and two, I needed a place to live. It was a full moon in November on a Friday night in Bozeman, Montana, and I needed to get to my sister's house who lived in Livingston twenty-five miles away. The only problem was that my stereo broke and it may as well have been a blown gasket because there was no way I was driving anywhere without a stereo.

I quickly ran to Walmart for something that fit my college budget and called my sister.

"It's only eight PM. I just have to put in a stereo quick and I'll head right over."

Six frustrating hours later, I still had no tunes in my van. I gave up. "It's only twenty-five miles," I thought to myself. Then I thought of the pioneers.

"Surely if they crossed the plains in covered wagons, I could drive twenty-five miles without tunes," I mumbled to myself, threw down my Phillips screwdriver and stared at my scared eyes in the review mirror. "I can do this," I whispered.

It was now 2 a.m. and I had the quiet highway to myself, but my mind was like a California rush hour freeway. It always is. The only thing that saves my mind from constant horns beeping, fender benders, road rage, and missed exits is music. Music is my mind's carpool lane and after listening to five minutes of tires rolling on the highway, I longed for it. I sang out loud to myself. "WE WILL, WE WILL ROCK YOU! Buddy, you're a bloob de bloop blah de da da"

Huh, I guess I only knew a few words to that song. I still had twenty miles to go. It was late, I needed something that rocked, and that song only burned up ten seconds. I thought of another song, "Pour Some Sugar On Me! I'm hot. Stuck at sea. Hey, hey, you and me something, something…"

Ahh, man. I don't know those lyrics either. I tried song after song, but the only thing I could get out was the chorus. I still had fifteen miles to go on this lonely highway and I was running out of songs. Then, I thought to myself, "What about church songs? Those things will never leave my head."

The first song I sang just about put me to sleep like it always did those Sunday mornings. What was I thinking? It was two in the morning, after all. But I DID know the lyrics, and it burned a few more miles. I tried another church song that had a little more pep in it.

"The Spirit of God, Like a Fire, is Burning!"

Oh yeah, I thought to myself as I sang the first line. This could work, but it needs to rock, so I got an idea. I sang another verse and honked my horn at the end of the verse. Oh yeah, that gave a nice touch. I hadn't seen one car since Bozeman, so it didn't matter. So, I sang the next verse loud and gave an even louder honk at the end. I was getting into it now and with each verse; I gave an even louder honk. Then came a verse that read, "We'll sing, and we'll shout!" and I yelled the word shout, lifted my right hand high with a metal fist into the air! I then pounded on that horn like it was a hammer to ring the bell at the county fair for a life-size teddy bear. And then…

"Hoooooooooooonkkkkkkkk"

I was wide awake now! Rock n Roll!

"Hooonnnkkkkk!"

Wait … what's happening? My van's horn was not stopping!

"Hooooooooonnnnkkkkkk!"

I couldn't believe it. My Chevy Astro van's horn was stuck. It was actually stuck! What do I do now?

"Hoooooooooonnnnnkkkkkk!"

I just couldn't imagine if a highway patrol officer sat parked, sipping on his coffee, in the middle of the night, in the middle of Montana, and saw a van driving down the highway with his horn blaring. How would I explain that?

"Hooooooonnnnnkkkk!"

My horn was still blaring, and I was frantic. I could not pull into Livingston at two in the morning and wake up the entire neighborhood. I could not just park it; the horn would still blare with the engine off. I drove for another mile or so with my horn blaring. Ten miles to go. The pressure was on. I only had a few minutes to figure this out. It didn't help that on a scale of zero to Arnold Schwarzenegger, my mechanical abilities were "Jingle All the Way". Not that good.

As the town of Livingston drew closer, I tried a last-ditch effort. I've heard of stories where sometimes adrenaline can give one superhuman strength. With my cruise control still set at 80, I reached behind the steering wheel and with all my strength ripped the horn cover off, and perhaps a miracle … the honking stopped. It stopped. For the first time in my life, I loved the quiet. The rest of the way to Livingston, I didn't sing a word; I didn't mumble a word; I didn't even think a word.

My mind was no longer racing like a California freeway but as peaceful as a 2 a.m. lonely Montana highway. I hired someone to install my car stereo the very next day.

# THE HIGH DIVE RIGHT OF PASSAGE

Certain cultures have unique rites of passage to become a man. For instance, the Vanuatu tribe of the South Pacific like to jump headfirst off a hundred-foot-high wooden tower with vines around their ankles onto solid ground. To become a man in the Sataré-Mawé tribe of the Brazilian Amazon, all you must do is put your hand in a glove full of the excruciating stings of bullet ants for ten minutes without making a noise. To become a man in the African Maasai tribe, you get to go fight a lion after mutilation of your "uume". Do your own translation. Well, not to be outdone, our Glendive City pool had its own rite of passage. If one wanted to play "Tag" and "Marco Polo" with the cool kids on the deep end, the only way was to first jump off the death-defying fifteen-foot-high dive.

I envision the high dive being built by some engineer who built all the other insurance rate-raising playground equipment. Even as a ten-year-old kid, I imagined the conversation.

"But boss … um … we are building these monkey bars over solid concrete. Won't that hurt if they fall?"

The boss, who was probably a World War vet who had seen the evils of the world and knew what to prepare the kids for, would reply.

102

"If they fall and break their arm, maybe they won't fall anymore. Just build it!"

It didn't stop at monkey bars over concrete either. We also had ten-foot metal slides. It is difficult to explain to the kids these days the joys and talent of sliding down a metal slide on a 100-degree July day in those 1980 short shorts. One false move of skin touching the metal slide, and you screech to a halt resulting in a third-degree burn for the week.

The teeter-totter was another favorite. NOT! Cody, my childhood friend, was twice as big as me. He later became an offensive lineman for the Wyoming Cowboys. Usually having a friend twice as big as me was an enormous advantage on the playground, but not with the teeter-totter. It was the price I had to pay.

Teeter totters gave me my first physics lesson. Cody would sit on the ground and laugh as my runt of the litter body held on like Lane Frost on Redrock. Then, without me knowing, he would thrust off the ground and my tailbone would freefall to the ground, then thrust right back into the air as Cody came gently back down. The higher Cody sent me up in the air on the other end, the more he would laugh. Those playground engineers were geniuses, all right. Nothing prepared us for life like a playground from the 80s.

I stared at that high dive and back at Cody and the gang. Being the runt of the gang, I always had to pull off the crazy stunts to earn their respect. Just jumping off would not do it. As I climbed up the fifteen-foot ladder, I thought to myself about the possibilities.

"A Cannonball? No ... that was Cody's signature move. The splash would never compare. A Jackknife? No ... that's too easy, anyone can do a Jackknife. A Swan Dive? The Running Man?"

I had one chance to impress the gang. I didn't want to blow it. As I stood shivering up in the wind, the best idea popped into my head. I got it! All the eyes were upon me and if I was ever going to play tag with the cool kids again, they better get something good. I ran off that high dive and jumped as high as I could. I then spread both my legs as far apart as if I was Bruce Lee. As soon as Cody saw my form, he knew exactly what I was going to do.

"No way!" Cody gasped. "He's doing the Dawson County Nutcracker!".

The eyes and mouths of my friends were all agape. I then pointed my toes. The toes had to be pointed. I pointed both hands to the sky and looked straight ahead. I was going for a perfect ten score. It felt like slow motion. The key was to hold the form until the end. Any movement of my legs would be a chicken out and thus no respect-points given.

Suddenly, I hit the water with a sound like the paddle from the principal's office.

"Whap!"

I knew by the sound and by my pain I had made a perfect ten. Cheers greeted my first breath of air. I did it! I became a man.

Year after year, that city pool high dive tested many kids, both girls and boys, of their bravery, preparing them for the real world. It was the ultimate litmus test for success in life. Then around 1991 something happened, and the world changed for the worse and I am not even talking about Nirvana.

Glendive, for some reason, took out the high dive! I screamed in horror as I drove by and saw it was missing. Fools! You have no idea what you have done! I knew what this would do to society. Suddenly, there were no more adults anymore. Everyone became easily offended, angered, and entitled. The beginning of the decline of Western Civilization happened right here, in Glendive, Montana, when they took out the high dive that sad day. That ol' World War veteran who built those monkey bars over concrete, the Maasai who mutilate their own "uume" and Sataré-Mawé who wear bullet ant gloves, all knew exactly what they were doing.

Sometime, in the not-so-distant future, an Archeologist will dig up our collapsed civilization and ask, "What happened? Where did it all go wrong?"

It was the high dive. It was the day Glendive removed the high dive.

# PURA VIDA!

"Pura Vida!" This was the first thing my brother Chris, and I learned on our trip to Costa Rica last week. "Pura Vida!" meaning "Pure Life." The Costa Ricans used this term to say hello, goodbye or just to send good vibes. It is the Tico (Costa Rican) way of life. Pura Vida is an attitude, a happiness that's difficult to describe until you have visited Costa Rica. Don't worry about the bad, don't stress about it, life is good, "Pura Vida!" Our first day was filled with magical, colorful, abundant wildlife and happy people. Costa Rica is an Eden, like a rare painting in a museum that's under the most careful care and protection. Chris caught on to the Pura Vida lifestyle right away. Whether it was the cashier at the "soda" (local eatery), our guide, or a police officer, Chris would yell out, "Pura Vida!"

It makes sense Chris would identify with this lifestyle. About fourteen years ago, my brother was hit on the head. The force of the hit burst a blood vessel in his brain, causing the blood to push his brain to the side. If the seriousness was attended to right away, Chris would have avoided the Traumatic Brain Injury. The good news was a saint by the name of Katrina noticed a few hours later and could get him to the hospital in the nick of time. The nick of time to be in a coma, anyway. He lay there motionless, caught in a void between life and death. It was the furthest thing from Costa Rica and "Pura Vida." It was more like a vacation to Chernobyl.

Our next few days in Costa Rica were full of more tropical magic. Crocodile tours, beaches, snorkeling, and plantains that tasted wonderful. Chris's brain works differently now. For instance, we would drive, and an American song would come on the radio. Chris would spew off verses word for word along with the radio. I can't even remember the lyrics to Happy Birthday. But late at night at a new hotel, I would see him enter the closet instead of the bathroom. Luckily, I was up and caught him before I lost my deposit from a deposit. He is also a former high school state tennis doubles champion. Winning state was easier for him to do back then than walking through an airport is now.

"I don't want to leave Costa Rica; I love it here!" Chris said to me as we were leaving a beach that he couldn't walk on because the sand got in his leg brace.

In the fourteen years since his coma, Chris has never once complained. I complain about how my life turned out every day, even though that is because of my own choices. Of course, he would fall in love with a country so full of life.

"Well, I have something special planned for you today," I replied.

I saw an ad saying, "Longest ocean view Superman-style zip line in Costa Rica!" I couldn't resist. That ad got me. We visited a zipline that was advertised as a mile long and eight stories high. The zipline spanned an enormous valley, all built by the lowest bidder. I could have told Chris it was a rocket ship to the moon, and he would have replied, "Pura Vida! Let's do it!"

As we made our way to the zipline, Chris turned to me laughing, "The guy in front of me just chickened out in front of his girlfriend!" It was true and Chris said it loud enough for him to hear it. Whether on purpose, I don't know.

As they put my zip-lining gear on, I reminded the local employee it was hard to tip if I didn't make it. I stepped on the scale and it read '99'. I love the metric system! Huh, I must not be fat anymore. The shuttle truck somehow made a steep climb to the top of the mountain, all in first gear. I think this was the most dangerous part.

"Donde pora vu!" Chris said to the local Tico as we put our lives in his hands. Chris was always making up Spanish words the whole trip, but he'd say them so confidently the locals would doubt their own Spanish. The zipline had two cables side by side so Chris and I could go together. The view of the Pacific Ocean and the deep rainforest valley looked magnificent.

I looked over at Chris. "You ready for this?" Chris gave a thumbs up. That thumbs up struck my memory of the last time Chris gave a thumbs up.

Fourteen years ago, as Chris lay motionless in his coma state for a few days, there was nothing our family could do. We went back to our jobs and lived as best we could with the unknown fate of our brother, while Mom and another family member took turns sitting with Chris.

Eight motionless days had now passed and not a peep from Chris. A piece of his skull was in a refrigerator, which allowed the swelling brain some room to heal. I still remember the day; our family called it Black Friday. I was up on a ladder working when my eldest brother Eric called. He said, "I just called to tell you we spoke to the doctor today. She told us that Chris will not make it. The damage is just too severe. Maybe a couple more days, then they will have to 'pull the plug'".

Eric continued, "The only person at the hospital who still believes is Mom". It was the toughest call to hear, but it was time to prepare for the worst. The next day, the doctors tried for a response one more time.

"Chris! Can you hear me? Are you there Chris?" And just like that thumbs up on the zipline, Chris gave the doctor his first sign of life—a thumbs up!

We both took off Superman-style down that mile-long zipline. The ninety-nine kilograms went by faster for me than for my younger brother. As we approached sixty miles per hour at eight stories high, I heard a shout from behind, "Pura Vida!"

Yes, Pura Vida indeed Chris. Pura Vida!

# THE REVENGE OF PAM

"Parker Brothers made Ouija Board? The same company that makes Chutes and Ladders?" I exclaimed to my friend Dave as we walked through the game aisle at White Drug.

"I thought the Ouija Board was supposed to be devilish?"

Dave's eyes grew large.

"Oh yes, it is! I've heard stories!"

Dave proceeded to rattle off about five strange Ouija board stories he had filed away in his brain.

"No Way…" I shot back. "It's a bunch of mumbo jumbo. Why would Parker Brothers be selling satanic stuff right here in White Drug?"

I looked at the game next to it. It was Monopoly. Now, THERE was a game from The Devil. Anyone who has ever landed on Park Place with a full hotel, only to roll snake eyes on the next turn and land on Boardwalk knows the complete depths of evil thoughts that can occur as you mortgage properties while your little brother dances around the table in sinister laughter with his little gluttonous finger pointed at you. Dave brought my attention back to him.

"Hey, should we play it tonight?" He said with a mischievous grin.

At eighteen years of age, Dave and I were like gas and fire when looking for things to do. There were no cell phones to entertain us. We spent the night before waiting and hiding at hole number three with bottle rockets because we heard a few friends were playing glow-in-the-dark golf. It worked. We hid in the sand bunker and scared the mulligans out of them. The week before that, we were lighting paper milk cartons on fire and watching them float down the river at night. Tonight, the entertainment was the Ouija board. (Parents, you can begin shaking your heads now).

We invited a few friends over and began asking a few dumb questions. The girls would ask who they would marry, the boys would ask who is going to the Super Bowl. I was a nonbeliever and sat and watched as the board would spell out the answers.

"You guys are moving it yourself!"

But they insisted, "We are not! It's moving on its own" they said with each hand touching the Ouija planchette.

Then, like typical eighteen-year-olds, the questions got a little darker.

"Is there somebody else in the room?" The board started spelling out letters. P.A.M. "Pam. Is your name Pam?" Just then a dog barked, and everyone screamed. Apparently, we had a ghost in the house named Pam.

"Oh, C'mon, that dog barks every fifteen minutes. Let me try," I said as I joined in. We started asking more questions for the sake of entertainment only.

We asked, "When will Dave Fuqua die?" The letters spelled out with anticipation. M.A.R.C.H 1.7.

"March 17th?" The planchette then moved to 'YES'.

"Ok, *how* will I die?" I asked in a snide voice.

Again, it spelled out K.N.I.F.E.

"Ok, whatever. This is stupid. Last question … By who?"

The letters started to once again spell out P.A.M.

"Pam! Pam's the killer?"

My friend Dave's eyes grew enormous.

"This thing is so dumb. I'm done." I left the entertainment for the night and went home. Next time I'll stick with the usual and just rent a VHS with the occasional blurry lines running through.

A few months later, with that Ouija night long forgotten, Dave and I were up to our usual eighteen-year-old shenanigans. We came home late past midnight and started preparing our usual late-night tradition: Strawberry milk, eggs, and toast. Dave got out the pan, eggs, and milk. He looked for a butter knife, but all the knives were in the dishwasher. The only knife Dave could find was this extra-long machete of a steak knife just to butter the toast. Then Dave looked at the pan. The worst thing in the world is eggs sticking to the pan. He reached for the Pam cooking spray. There, Dave stood with a large knife in one hand and Pam in the other.

"Do you like your eggs scrambled?" He asked with the knife in one hand and Pam in the other.

This jolted a faint Ouija memory of a few months ago. "Knife. Pam?" I thought? No way. I held my breath and glanced at my Casio watch. I focused on the date. It was after midnight and the official date was MARCH 17TH!

"Dave. Look!" as I showed him my watch. "It's March 17th!"

"Yeah, so what?" He replied.

I pointed at the machete-butter knife in his right hand and then the Pam cooking spray in his left. It suddenly clicked in Dave's brain as both our eyes grew large and we screamed in each other's faces like a couple of schoolgirls.

"It's PAM! AHHHHHHHHHH!" We continued to scream as Dave dropped the objects from his hand and we both ran out the door at two in the morning. This story could not be truer. Out of breath, and our hearts racing, I whispered to Dave, "I didn't know ghosts had such a good sense of humor. She got us good!"

# ATTENTION PLEASE!

I had just missed the turn to the Bozeman, Montana Walmart for the third time in a row, not because of the Bozeman traffic problem, but because of a Dave daydreaming problem. For example, the week before, I went to the bank to cash a check. I sent the check through the tube that mysteriously disappeared into another dimension to a distant teller stuck behind a glass window, just like the primate encounter I saw at the Denver Zoo. I smiled and waved to the teller and took off while completely forgetting to take my money. It was a reverse bank robbery.

Sometimes, I also like to do that at the Wendy's drive-through. The week before that, I had just washed my recently purchased Grand Am for the first time in six months. I then went grocery shopping and when I came back out to the full parking lot, I had to walk around the lot three times before I finally found my car. I walked past it twice, not recognizing it.

A couple months before that, I went to eat at the local Chinese buffet. I was by myself and in a hurry and put that 'chicken lo mein' down like I had a pack of wild dogs waiting to steal it if I did not finish in time. Then, while still in a hurry, my next errand was to go to Applebee's and get a gift certificate I had promised an employee. The bartender was an amazingly attractive girl.

I smiled my best smile and asked, "Hi, I just need to get a gift certificate. Could you do that for me?" Bartenders usually smile and are polite, but this particularly attractive girl gave me the most stone-faced horrid look. I stopped smiling immediately.

"Am I that ugly? She won't even smile?"

She wrote out the gift certificate stone-faced, and she didn't say a word during the entire transaction. I was miffed, with a thousand thoughts of what could be wrong, as I walked back through the parking lot to my car. I got in, put the car in reverse, and checked the rear-view mirror. Then came the revelation. Staring back at me in the mirror, the shape of a capital "S", was the largest lo mein noodle I had ever seen clinging to my goatee beard like Velcro!

A couple of years ago, I went for my nightly walk in the neighborhood of my hometown of Glendive. This is the same hometown that rarely gets their water bill paid because they only accept handwritten checks. Apparently, Glendive also still wishes it was 1987. This night was the Fourth of July. I only meant to walk to the park and back, which would normally take a few minutes.

"Ka-zing! BOOM! Crackle!" With all the fireworks and bright colors around me, I stopped and stared and then stopped and stared some more. I got back home an hour later, and realized, "Oh my Gosh … this is my brain! I can't get anywhere sometimes, because my thoughts are like fireworks. Always shooting, always firing, on and on, but none seem to lead anywhere!"

The only words I remember from my eighth-grade shop teacher were this:

"Fuqua! You are so dense sometimes!" He had just finished giving me directions, but his directions were so boring I drifted off thinking about the snowman I was going to build at recess during his second sentence when he said something about "measuring with a ruler".

So, after missing the turn to Walmart for the third straight time, an ad came on my radio. It was for a product named "Focus Factor".

An excited voice blared through the radio. "Do you sometimes have trouble remembering where you put the keys?!"

"Oh yeah," I thought.

"Last summer, I put my keys in the cereal cupboard. I had to ride my bike for a few days until I used up all the eggs and had to eat cereal for breakfast again."

The voice on the radio excitingly blared again, "Do you lose things easily?"

"Wow … how do they know? Just last week I searched for thirty minutes for my sunglasses. I found them on top of my head!"

The commercial said one more thing that closed the deal. "Do you often wait until the last minute to do a project?"

I can't tell you how many gas station Christmas gifts my family gets.

"If this is YOU, please call 1-800-FOCUS FACTOR!"

I dug through the trash in that crack between my car seat and the center console to find my phone while simultaneously flipping the U-turn back towards Walmart. I dialed the number as fast as I could. This product could change my life.

"Hello, Focus Factor—"

"Can you hold please?" and without even hearing my response, they sent me to elevator music.

"Hold?" I shouted in frustration as I took the phone away from my ear and stared at it like it just asked a fish if it minded being on land for a minute. Needless to say, they missed the sale.

Luckily for me, I told my older brother about this product, and he drew my name for the next Christmas. I unwrapped his gift and there in my hand was the largest bottle of Focus Factor I had ever seen. My life was about to change, I thought. Oh, the books that I will write. My house will always be clean. My bills will always be paid, and my wallet will never be lost! I will never forget anything again! The list went on and on.

But, to my dismay, that bottle of Focus Factor pills never got used. It still sits unopened in a cluttered drawer somewhere today. I could never remember to take the pill.

# THE FROG WHO SAVED CHRISTMAS

Christmas mornings typically brim with wondrous moments. Christmas of '77', it was a Big Wheel. In '80' it was a Millennium Falcon. And in '94' (at that adult time in my life), it was wondrous socks and underwear. The Christmas of 2013, however, I woke up to another wondrous sight. It was a cute frog in my toilet. I was in the part of the Amazon Jungle that stretched to eastern Ecuador. Everything about spending December 25th in the jungle was the antithesis of Christmas. Santa lived in the North Pole. I was on the equator. In Montana, the snow sparkled off the moonlight on those Christmas Eve nights as if Mother Nature had a two-year-old who dumped a bottle of glitter. My Amazon Christmas night was not white but filled with amazing fluorescent fireflies, as if I was in the movie Avatar.

Instead of a quiet evergreen winter forest, the jungle was an animal party every night decorated with monkey howls and occasional roars. Some friends and I spent Christmas that year in the Amazon. It was an amazing tour. We held caiman gators with our bare hands; fished for piranha; hunted (with no success) for an anaconda; spotted sloths, pink dolphins, toucans, monkeys, and spiders the size of Wyoming. You name it; we saw it.

On Christmas Day, I woke up to a frog in my toilet.

Never have I come upon such a stalemate in my life as a frog in a toilet. What could I do? Nature called. The frog was cute. I couldn't do my business on the frog, and I didn't dare reach in and grab it. I just stood there and stared. The frog did the same to me. Every decision I had ever made in my life, right or wrong, had led me to Christmas morning in the Amazon, staring at a frog in the toilet. What do you do with a frog in the toilet? I stared at the amphibian longer. I then thought, maybe this frog was my own Christmas fable. We all grew up with Frosty the Snowman or Rudolph the Red-Nosed Reindeer. How about Dave and the Amazon Toilet Frog on Christmas morning? I wondered if the Hallmark channel paid royalties. Three ghosts visited Ebenezer to remind him of what Christmas was all about. Maybe a frog visited me in a toilet bowl to remind *me* of what Christmas was about.

What was I doing in the jungle on Christmas, anyway? Everything I had ever associated with Christmas was completely absent. No snow, no Christmas trees, no lights.

No Mariah Carey's "All I Want for Christmas is You" playing on the radio 24/7!

Ok, it wasn't all bad after all. Nevertheless, what have I become? Christmas used to be my favorite holiday as a child. Then, slowly, with each year, the hustle, the stress, the Black Fridays, and the whirlwind of Christmas had chipped away the childhood nostalgia of Christmas year by year until finally Christmas just felt like a jungle.

Perhaps I finally ended up where I thought I belonged on Christmas. In a jungle. I stared at the frog again and reached for the handle to give it a flush. It was my best solution.

I whispered, "Sorry, frog, but it's a frog-eat-frog world out there!"

With my hand on the handle, I paused. No. Not on Christmas. I can't flush a frog on Christmas Day.

I backed off and decided for the sake of the frog to use the public head by the mess hall. As I walked to the dining room area, the rest of the tour group was already eating breakfast.

"Merry Christmas, Dave!" Lucas from Holland cheered. "Did you come bearing gifts?"

"Well ... sort of," I replied with an inside smirk.

I then looked around. There was Xiu Ying from China, Reyansh from India, Steven from Utah, Lucas and his brother from Holland, and Maria from Chile. The list went on and on. I had only known these people from all over the world for a week, yet here we were, all eating a Christmas breakfast peacefully and happily, as if we were one big family. We had zero communication with the rest of the world.

Whatever turmoil and wars among nations existed in the world did not exist here. I made instant friends from all corners of the globe who all just wanted to experience an amazing world. It was Kyrie among nations. It was truly 'Peace on Earth and Goodwill Toward Men'.

May we all find frogs in our toilets this Christmas morning!

# FAST TIMES AT DAWSON HIGH

Some kids grow up as paupers, some kids grow up as princes. But some, the luckiest of them all, grew up kitty-corner from Dawson County High School during written history's greatest decade. This kid was me. John Cougar Mellencamp's "Jack and Diane," blasted out of a Burt Reynolds wannabe Trans-Am at least once a day, accompanied by a squeal of the tires. Aqua-net stock was on the rise and kids would walk by with 'The Empire Strikes Back' shirts while the Rose Theater finally showed it six months later. Yes, the Litmus test said "1982".

These were action-packed fast times at Dawson High. I'd always make sure I was outside playing when the last bell of the day rang. "Smokers Ally", the hangout for the kids who lettered in smoking, was only ten feet from my swing set. I would try to listen in and sometimes learn a new word for the day. The smoker kids sure must like Italian food because they would always talk about marinara.

If I was lucky, I'd even get to witness a fight or two. Then I would look for the "Brown Shadow". Grant, who lived a block away, never walked by without his hot girlfriend close behind him, whose last name was Brown. Sometimes I would press my face against the screen door and make my nose look like a pig as the kids walked by. Guaranteed laughs from everyone. Sometimes the marching band would practice

"We Got the Beat," marching around my block with some girl in front throwing a stick in the air whose only purpose was just to get our attention. That's all it took to get our attention in the 80s; a girl throwing a stick in the air. I would follow that band around the block in my totally awesome big-wheel Green Machine. If you don't know what a Green Machine is, just google "Big Green Sexy Toy" and you'll see what I'm talking about. Anyway, growing up across from the high school as a wide-eyed ten-year-old boy was everything I could ask for.

There was one day that stood out in particular. I heard a large teenager cackling from a crowd across the street. I threw down my hot wheel and ran towards the window in a Pavlovian response to the high school excitement. There, in the middle of Kendrick Ave, was a large circle of high schoolers, all hollering, laughing, screaming and cackling.

"It's *go* time!" I thought and ran out the door to see what today's high school action was about.

By the way, don't google "Big, Green Sexy Toy" to see what a Green Machine looks like. I just did that, and it didn't turn out how I planned. Anyway, I ran to the circle of high schoolers and weaved my way under the legs to the middle to see what the commotion was about. In the center of the crowded circle was a half-dead bull snake clinging to life. The boys would kick it or mess with it, and each time, the crowd would scream. This snake was in trouble and after watching Marlin Perkins of Mutual of Omaha's "Wild Kingdom" wrestle a twenty-five-foot Anaconda, and "Beastmaster" the week before, I knew exactly what to do. I jumped in and grabbed the bull snake by the back of the neck with my left hand and the rest of the body with my right. Then the crowd gave the biggest roar yet!

As I noticed all the adoring eyes of the cool high school kids upon me, my ten-year-old ego inflated. The attention grabbed me by the back of the neck the same way I held the snake. I lost all control of my once altruistic motivations towards this poor bull snake. As the cheers grew louder, my ego got bigger. In that moment, I may as well have been Gene Simmons. I'll never have to put my nose to the screen door again. I think I saw the Brown Shadow take her eyes off Grant for a minute and twinkle her eyes at the ten-year-old beast master.

With all eyes on me, I raised the snake above my head and yelled, "ARE YE NOT ENTERTAINED!" and the crowd roared! (OK, I'm exaggerating a bit, but not that much). I snapped out of my moment of glory and focused back on the poor snake. I started moving through the crowd with the dying snake in my hands and they parted like the Red Sea as I headed home. Luckily, we had an empty trashcan available just like the one Oscar the Grouch lived in, and I set the snake down safely. It was barely moving.

Mom saw me and screamed. "How do you know that's not a rattlesnake!!"

"Geez, mom!" I hissed back, "I know the difference, I'm not an idiot!" I didn't really know the difference.

Miraculously, Oscar the snake made a full recovery after about a month in the trashcan. I took Oscar down by the creek at the Little League fields and tearfully set him free. There was no Snapchat, Instagram, or Facebook to document it like kids have these days. Just a Firebird driving by in the distance playing John Cougar Mellencamp. "Oh Yeah, life goes on … long after the thrill of living is gone…"

# D-O-G SPELLED BACKWARD

I reached into that plastic bag and held it like a puppet. "This is so backward!" I thought to myself. We are supposed to be the masters, yet here I am picking up after my brother's dog, Fred. I grimaced, held my breath, and leaned over the long grass with my patented move of grabbing the full-grown black lab's recycled dinner with an inside-out bag. Sometimes it took two. I tried not to look too closely, but this time I saw something peculiar. There were words!

I grew up with dogs on the silver screen. Lassie, Shaggy D.A., even Scooby Doo. Hollywood has programmed me since childhood that dogs are special. Heroic. They all go to heaven. Yet here I was with Fred. I looked again curiously at the magical words surrounded by a bit of steam. "C-A-L-V," and then I couldn't make out the rest. They started up again, "K-L-E," then faded into brown oblivion.

At first, I thought Fred was magic. "Could my brother have a magic dog? Is this the winner of tomorrow's football game? Is he spelling out my future? Will I have to drop extra pepperoni on the floor tonight to find the rest of the message tomorrow?"

Once again, I thought of all those Hollywood dog movies I grew up with. This is one plot I have not seen before. I thought more about those letters. What could they mean? I wondered what the neighbors thought as they saw me staring at Fred's poop in the middle of the park like it was an Algebra II final.

I spelled it out in my mind again, "C-A-L-V, K-L-E, Calvin? Calvin Klein? The Underwear? No Way! He ate my brother's underwear?

"I had so many questions. How does this pass through him? Why would this taste good? Since when did my fashion-less brother go GQ with Calin Klein? Yet, there it was, in its plain lettering. My brother's dog ate his master's underwear. I thought about leaving it, just so a fifth-grade boy could see it and have an amazing story to tell at school.

But then I thought about all the times I made a diving grab in the park for a football. More times than not, I got more than a grass stain on my pants. I decided I had better double bag this one and did my civic duty while Fred was off rolling around in the grass in who knows what else. I walked Fred back to the house bewildered at his digestive system and how backward the situation was. Fred followed behind me, just as happy as ever. He just ate a pair of Calvin Klein underwear and seemed to be the happiest thing I had ever seen. The moment felt more backward than ever.

Backward. I thought again. Perhaps I was missing something. Maybe we are living backward. What if the word DOG was spelled backward? What lessons would I learn? I remember one of the last times I saw my amazing family friend Dennis Getz before his untimely passing. He was playing in the yard with his dogs, having the best time.

Dennis looked at me and said, "One lesson I learned from a dog is the only thing you need to be happy is a stick."

I never forgot that. I came up with a few other lessons from a dog if DOG was spelled backward.

1. Let everyone you meet see your tail wagging.

2. As you take your walk-through life, leave your mark everywhere.

3. Do not go through life rolling over for people, but if you do, make sure treats are involved.

4. Sniff out the butts right away so you can stay away from them.

5. You don't have to love on every single leg. Some legs kick.

6. Nobody likes a beggar. Act with dignity and your bowl will be full.

7. A peaceful home has learned to make sure its crap is left outside the home.

8. The loyal and loving get to share half the master's bed, the ones that bite get the pound.

9. Be careful who you get "nuder" for. The wrong choice and you will find you have gone nuts.

I haven't seen any magic words come out of Fred's bum for a long time. Maybe someday I will sell the movie rights to Disney. (I am thinking naturally, the star of the movie is going to be a Shih Tzu.)

As a child, most of my life's lessons I learned from the outcome of tales. Now, as an adult, I realize my life's lesson came from the outcome of a tail.

# DIFFUSING THE MARTHA STEWART BOMB

Remember the term "Curse like a sailor?" Somehow, like a virus, the sailor vernacular has spread to the everyday lingo of our latest generation of kids around the turn of this century and they are ruining it. That word is no longer a bomb, but mere BB's because of how often it's used, thus losing the word's power. I was there in the spring of 2000 when the foul vernacular first spread. After graduating by the skin of my teeth with a biology degree, I applied for an intriguing job in Alaska as a "fisheries observer" among the fishing boats of the unforgiving Bering Sea. The job required a biology degree, but I found out later, like most jobs, graduating from kindergarten would have been sufficient. One fish, two fish, red fish, blue fish. That was literally about all I did. One Dr. Seuss book was all I needed to read.

As I boarded my first boat from Dutch Harbor, they smelled the greenhorn on me like sharks on a sardine. Before I could even set my bags in my cabin, the Chief Engineer ordered, "Hey! You need to watch that hatch right now to make sure it doesn't overflow!"

"O ... Kaaay?" I curiously replied.

It made little sense, but I wanted to make friends right away, so I did what I was told. I guarded that hatch closely. A screw-up during my first fifteen minutes on board would be a disaster.

Twenty minutes went by. "How we doing?" I impatiently asked.

"Keep watching!" He crustily replied with every stereotype of an old fisherman.

Another fifteen minutes went by, and my suspicions finally clicked in my mind. "There isn't any water in here, is there?" as the crew started cracking up at their first prank towards the greenhorn. It turned out to be the hatch where they kept the fish.

"Martha Stewart!" I muttered to myself, but the chief heard it and I explained sheepishly.

"I'm not really a swearer, so sometimes I say Martha Stewart instead of a swear word."

The chief looked at me like I was the strangest thing he had ever seen in his thirty years at sea. A barrage of his original versions of "Martha Stewarts" immediately followed.

We had a two-day steam to get to our turbot fishing grounds off the Pribilof Islands, two hundred miles north of Dutch Harbor. Confined to a boat with twenty guys, this is when I could truly witness "curse like a sailor," in all its glory. I could barely communicate with them. Every pronoun, noun, verb, adverb, adjective, and sometimes even conjunctions from the more talented were all shall we say "Martha Stewarts". It was the same word over and over. Yet, somehow, they understood each other perfectly. It was all in the inflection. I read somewhere that the Chinese have words that sound the same. The only difference in changing the meaning was how you said those words. This is how the fisherman communicated. Sometimes, I would speak complete, articulate sentences with no color to them. They would just stare at me like I stared at my engine under the hood when my car broke down.

The next day, I spent some time with the captain on the bridge. Somehow, the captain could speak without adding "Martha Stewarts." All his fishing stories fascinated me. I soaked it up. Finally, after a two-day steam, we neared the Pribilof fishing grounds. Turbot was selling in Japan at a price as high as the crews' spirits. I was up on the bridge with the captain. He must have run out of stories, or he was immersed in fishing anticipation because we both stood there quietly. Then, suddenly, the captain yelled the loudest, most intense shriek of a "Martha Stewart" I had ever heard. It was the first time he swore during the entire trip. The word pierced the quiet air like lightning in a July storm. The word struck me to the core as if he just threw a grenade. He was so brash; I just wanted to suck my thumb and hide behind a blanket.

"What! What?" I was almost afraid to ask.

He just pointed towards the starboard side. For the captain, it was the equivalent of getting approached by a couple of thugs in a dark alley with a wallet full of cash. For me, it was a magnificent sight that I'll never forget. Two long black fins, males, to be exact, swimming at the same speed next to the boat. "Orcas!" If I had shown my inner excitement, the captain would have thrown me overboard.

To the fisherman, orcas are nothing but thieves. They literally robbed them by biting off everything but the head from the long-lining boat. Hook after hook would only bring up a fish head, leaving the crew penniless. I, however, was getting paid regardless, and being surrounded by a pod of Killer Whales all day was like having my very own private Sea World and, —I didn't have any fish to count! It's no wonder sailors and fishermen swear so much. I, however, learned it is more effective to curse like a captain than swear like a sailor. I wish today's generation knew what power they would have if they only used the word sparingly, like the captain. The rest of this fish story is fascinating, and I promise I will tell it another day—I swear!

# COSTCO SAMPLE DICTATORS

In the back of my freezer, there are still teriyaki bowls from the purchase in May 2016. The corner of my cupboard above my stove still has Paleo bars left over from the purchase in August 2015. In my fridge door, there is a bottle of ketchup big enough for every hotdog sold at Fenway during a Yankee game from the purchase in December 2017. Twice a year, like a freshman who indulges too much at a frat homecoming party, I sometimes think it is a good idea to shop at Costco.

It all started a few years ago when my brother asked if I wanted to go to Costco with him. With his nose slightly in the air, he showed his own special membership card with his own picture on it.

"You can't shop there unless you go with me." He said as if he was Paris Hilton in the VIP line of Vegas's hottest nightclub.

Apparently, this store is so amazing, you have to pay thirty dollars a year, just to get by Nancy, the bouncer at the door. I showed up with my brother, but my ego caved. I, too, wanted to feel like Paris Hilton, so I went and paid thirty bucks for a card with my face on it. My posture straightened as a new confidence radiated as I walked past Nancy, flashing my new club card. If only any of my former high school teachers could see me now. They would be so surprised that I had finally made it.

I had no idea what I was shopping for, but I pushed the cart the size of a water buffalo anyway, as I bypassed the big-screen TVs, books, and clothes and headed straight for the samples. I see sample egg rolls! Free egg rolls! No wonder people pay thirty bucks a year. Does Paris Hilton get free egg rolls at her favorite Vegas club? I think not. With my cart still empty, I bolted for the egg rolls. But to my dismay, they were a hot item and Edith, the sample lady, was still cooking them. Edith caught me out of the corner of her eye, and with a coy voice said, "They are not quite ready yet, young man. Another couple of minutes."

"Oh, C'mon Edith," I murmured to myself. I pay thirty bucks a year for you to get your egg rolls right. I paced back and forth, not knowing if I could wait a whole two more minutes for Edith to get it together. I paced a bit more, and then the bell of the toaster rang.

Finally! Edith, however, wasn't finished making her chess move. She saw how I paced, and she doubled down. Throughout the history of Earth, rulers in different dispensations have usurped all their power unto their masses. Genghis Kahn, Alexander the Great, Napoleon, and now Edith. This was Edith's time of power. She saw me pace; she saw me eye those egg rolls, and she heard the toaster bell ring.

But Edith did not put that egg roll on the sample tray for me. With a snarky smirk, she slowly cut each egg roll, one by one, onto her own tray. They would be made available for consumption when Edith says they are ready. It was the most powerful Edith had ever felt in her life, and she milked it. I then made my own chess move. I would NOT give Edith the satisfaction, so I bounced to the next sample while she slowly cut those egg rolls in half. The next booth was some disgusting health drink thing. Whatever … it was free, and I intended to get all my membership perks.

"Thank you, that was pretty good! Where are those again?"

I totally lied. I'd never buy that stuff. I turned my attention back to Edith and the egg rolls. Surely, they would be ready by now. They were out, but they were disappearing fast. I quickened my pace. I was almost there when I gave a slow-motion "NOOOOOOOOOOO!" The last egg roll of the batch ... gone! I was too late. Snatched by another club member. Well played Edith. You got me this time ... but I'll be back, Edith, I'll be back.

I picked out a couple of things just because I was there and should probably buy something. Looks like I had better get used to eating frozen waffles and peanut butter for the next eighteen months. The checkout line looked like the line at Space Mountain. But the Costco Cashiers were amazingly efficient.

Before I knew it, the cashier snapped at me, "Two hundred and fourteen dollars! And we do not take that kind of credit card either!"

But I only bought five items! "Can I get a bag? Or do I just make five trips to the car?"

She gave me a look my mom used to give when I made sense, but she just didn't want to deal with me.

"No!" was the cashier's hard reply, and she was on to the next patron in line.

The confidence I had earlier showing Nancy my club pass had now disappeared. It was at that moment I saw the largest sign advertising a hot dog and a pop for only a buck fifty! A Dollar fifty! Don't do it, Dave! I don't even want to know what those things are made of. The fat, the grease, the preservatives, the calories. There was absolutely, positively, no way I would put that thing in my body!

Two minutes later, I had a line of relish on that thing that looked like I was backstage at the Ozzy Osborn, "Bark at the Moon" tour. I thought ... I could now live off of a dollar fifty a day. No ... I have to get out of here. This isn't a club; this is a cult.

I ran for the door.

"Do you have your receipt?"

Oh, for the love of Pete! I searched every pocket. This place is a cult. They won't even let me leave. I left the receipt by my hotdog, so I snatched my receipt and raced for the door. I tore out of those double-lined parking spaces so fast that all my unbagged items scattered in the trunk. It was too late. I'd been brainwashed. I can't wait to see Nancy's face next year when I upgrade to the Business card!

# SLEDDING TALES OF BROKEN TAILS

Moon boots. A one-piece bright yellow snowsuit. A ski mask that would terrify any modern bank teller. This was all the armor needed for a typical nine-year-old to survive a 1981 Glendive Montana winter. And let's not forget the oversized mittens. The same mittens that were padded enough to use as boxing gloves in the summer. Most importantly, like a knight and his trusty steed, a Montana kid needed a trusty sled. Sledding was life in the winter. We didn't have HD TVs. MTV wasn't on our cable yet. Our best video game (which I couldn't afford to pay a quarter for anyway) consisted of a large yellow half-circle consuming smaller yellow circles.

Needless to say, I spent my winter days entertained by sledding. Each neighborhood in Glendive had its own hill. I used Lloyd Park to the creek. The Heights had the coulee. Hillcrest used a street. Southside had to dodge the rocks in the Badlands, and Forest Park? Well, they didn't have a hill, but lucky for them they had enough oil roughnecks with three-wheelers to pull them around on their sleds.

These neighborhood hills were like Los Angeles gangs and their turf. If you were to go sledding on another neighborhood's hill, you better be prepared to fight for it. However, Glendive had one hill, the mother of all hills, where all neighborhoods were invited. My friend Brandon would tell me about it.

"Dave, we have to get our parents to take us to Camel's Hump!"

"Camel's Hump?" I replied, "Where is that?"

He explained further, "It's the biggest, baddest hill in Glendive. It takes like an hour to hike to the top, but the ride is forever! I bet it's better than the Matterhorn!"

It intrigued me.

I asked my mom if she would take us to Camel's Hump the next Saturday.

"So that means you and your brothers will all be away from the house all day?" She replied with heightened enthusiasm.

"Absolutely!"

Saturday came, and she dropped us off at Camel's Hump, which was littered with unsupervised kids all having the time of their life. That's the way parenting could be done back then. No texts or communication. Just be back when the streetlights come on. I think all the 80s moms had a secret spa or place they met every day that closed when the streetlights came on that modern moms know nothing about.

Anyway, looking up at Camel's Hump for the first time was like Sir Edmund Hillary looking at Everest. It was everything Brandon said it was, and more. My breath was as visible as the exhaust from the three-wheeler pulling kids up the hill. It didn't matter. The enormity of the incline spawned adrenaline that warmed my veins.

We started the trek upwards. I was so jealous of the three-wheel kids getting a ride up the hill, but Lloyd's kids didn't dare talk to the tough Forest Park kids.

Our expedition finally made the summit where there were a bunch of other kids all in ski masks, standing and waiting their turn. It looked like a bank robbers convention for little people.

"You guys just going just stay up here all day or what?" I asked the smallest kid, halfway expecting a turf war.

"Dave?" He shot back.

"Mark? That you? Mark?"

"Dave? That you? It's me, Bob!"

"BOB!" Mark and I simultaneously shot back.

Then another kid turned around. "Mark? Dave? Bob? It's Tyler!"

"TYLER? Hey, it's Tyler!"

We all couldn't believe everyone from town was here. With everyone wearing ski masks back then, nobody knew who anybody was during wintertime. Now, every kid had a different sled. Bob had a saucer. Pffft … a saucer! His parents actually bought him a sled that you have absolutely no control over. You'd just spin and meander down the hill. It was the worst sled ever invented. That sled would be symbolic of the rest of Bob's life.

Then, Tyler from the south side had a Kmart cheap roll-up sled. Mark from Hillcrest had a wooden sled with two razor-sharp guillotines underneath it.

"What is that?" I asked Mark.

He said his mom had it while she was growing up. I was only ten, but I was smart enough to know why the world's population escalated once kids stopped using the runner sled.

Now, the Lloyd Park kids had the absolute best sled of all time. The orange plastic toboggan. As Tina Turner would say, it was simply the best. Our boxing glove mittens made perfect rudders for steering and brakes if we needed them. And if you didn't have a torn-up, beat-to-heck orange plastic toboggan by March, you were doing it wrong.

We all played "Ketchup and Mustard". I went first as the mustard and the other kids had to "Catch up" in order to win. Camel's Hump was at just the right incline to go as fast as you wanted to. I went for it. I kept my boxing glove mittens inside my sled. Bob and his saucer had no chance. He spun around backward right away and drifted off to the side of the hill. I'm not sure if we saw him again that day. Mark and his personal guillotine zipped past me right away. That's ok, I could pass his blood stains later down the hill.

My trusty orange plastic toboggan was giving me the ride of my life when suddenly a ramp from nowhere thrust me into the air! I tumbled in the snow like a Saturday morning cartoon. With a few stars in my head, I looked upward and assessed my sledding obsession. The half-hour trek up the hill. The frost-bit toes and the half-broken tailbone. Are these Montana winters really worth it? I hobbled over to my sled and started walking back up Camel's Hump. Absolutely!

# THE CALM AFTER THE STORM

A few years ago, Montana had a dreadful dry year with devastating summer forest fires. That same summer, Houston had immense flooding with a heavy dose of rain from Hurricane Harvey. When this happened, I couldn't help but think. *What if there just happened to be some guy … who had just flown into Houston from Montana, prayed for rain, but forgot to say where?* Boy, would they feel like an idiot. That stormy thought brought up a memory.

I have a friend, Jason, whose hobby is mountain climbing. He always had great stories to tell at parties. My hobby was collecting rocks. Nobody talked to me at parties, well, except for Larry, whose hobby was making dream catchers. Larry thought I was fascinating, but I wanted to be more like Jason. I was in my late twenties and up to that point, I had accomplished little in my life.

"Maybe I should climb a mountain like Jason?" I thought.

"What better way to accomplish something while accomplishing nothing than to climb a mountain?"

Climbing a mountain will have zero relevance to the world but mean everything to my foundationless ego. It was exactly what a twenty-something man needed.

Just then, Jason, in the middle of one of his stories, said, "Yeah, me and a buddy are going to climb Granite Peak next week."

Now, Granite Peak is the highest peak in Montana. Anybody knows that if you truly want to be a man, climbing the highest peak in Montana is the measure of that. Not knowing what I was getting into, I spoke up,

"Hey if you need a third, I've always wanted to do that."

Jason laughed at first, then his eyes got big.

"Oh, you're serious, Dave!"

I wasn't serious—I was just a good actor—people were watching.

Of course, Jason was going to say, "No". Anyway, I figured it's like when beginning tennis players ask me to play tennis. Larry gave me a look as if I was a god.

"That's one crazy rock collector!" he thought.

"Ok, Dave," Jason replied to my surprise, "I'll get you a list of what you need. Do you have any carabiners?"

"What's a carabiner?" I could see Jason's disgust with my reply, but it was too late. We had both committed.

The 12,800-foot Granite Peak is best climbed in late August because of the rough mountain weather. I needed some warm snow pants (which I had none) so I asked my brother-in-law who was a mountain climber if he had any. He brought out these nice wool pants that were his favorite. I tried them and they fit great, but I did not walk in them. This was a great mistake, as we shall learn.

After driving all night with Jason and his friend, we arrived at the Mystic Lake trail and slept in our car until morning. The goal was to hike up the 3000-foot switchbacks and camp that night above the 10,000-foot elevation plateau.

We left early in the morning and didn't arrive until evening. I knew Jason and his friend were wary of hiking with a rookie. I pushed it hard and gained their confidence by the time we reached the plateau. It was incredibly exhausting. I tried not to let it show, but my early retirement to the tent gave me away. After all, today was easy, nothing technical. I needed a good night's sleep for tomorrow's ascent. I was getting nervous because there was going to be some technical climbing that I had no idea how to do. Granite Peak glared at us from our camp. It stood majestic and intimidating. I had no idea what I was getting myself into. The smart thing to do would be to check my ego at the door and let them go ahead, but by my late twenties I had become so good at getting away with dumb things, it became second nature. I was going to go for it!

That morning, we woke up, and I was told to put on my snow pants. It's going to get cold. Granite Peak loomed over us like a dragon ready to slay its next victim. I put on my brother-in-law's wool pants like a suit of armor. Jason and his buddy led the way, and I followed. Ten steps in, and "Whoop!" The nice wool pants were around my butt. Uh oh. I tried these pants on, but I did not WALK in them.

This was concerning. I pulled my pants up and in another three steps "DROOP". They were around my butt again.

"Oh, no … this is not good!" I thought.

I got a rhythm. Every third step, I'd swoop my pants up with my left hand. 1-2-3, droop and swoop. 1-2-3, droop and swoop.

"Ok. I can do this, only five or six more hours to go."

I looked back and camp was only two hundred yards away. 1-2-3, droop and swoop. I was still keeping up with Jason and his buddy. Granite Peak stared me in the face the whole time. My oxygen-deprived angel on my left shoulder started talking.

"Ok, this time I am really going to die. This is stupid, Dave, just be a man and turn back to camp!"

The devil on my right whacked him with a carabiner.

"That's not being a man!" and the devil won again.

I kept up with the droop and swoop method for another quarter mile, wondering how I could get out of this situation.

Then, literally out of the blue, as if I was David bleeping Copperfield, clouds formed among the torrent climate of the high elevation. It started to blizzard! Solid white was everywhere! It was glorious. Jason stopped with the same disgusted face he had when I asked if I could go with him.

"I hate to say this, guys, but we have to turn back."

Jason turned around with a heavy heart, but my heart was flying 12,800 feet high.

"Ahh ... serious! Well, if you think so."

I should have been an actor, but after a couple hundred more yards of droop and swoops, I couldn't hide it anymore. A happy rookie serenaded the dejected, serious mountain climbers the rest of the way back to camp.

"Oh, the weather outside is frightful ... Let it snow, let it snow, let it snow!"

# WHEN PIGS FRY

"De boat to da Amazon Rain Forest, leave in one hour!" The Ecuadorian guide said to us in a thick Latino accent. I couldn't wait. I usually judge my vacations on a scale of one to Indiana Jones, and this was going to be a full-on Temple of Doom. The only problem was it was a bit commercial. Like the TV show Survivor, my friends and I waited to get on the boat with ten other strangers whom I'd never met before. Soon, we will all be deep inside the Amazon Rain Forest for four days, knowing nothing about anyone and zero background checks. I've seen this movie before.

As we all waited, we chatted to get to know each other a little better. As dangerous as the rainforest can be, humans can be far more dangerous. So far, everyone was friendly, funny, and great. There was a nice Dutch family who was high in the government. They checked out. A couple of Asian blogger gals made a joke about everything. I liked them immediately. I even told one of them later.

"You just might be the funniest girl I have ever met." I thought it was a compliment, but I then learned another valuable female lesson.

She immediately retorted, "I do not want to be funny!" In her thick Asian accent, "I want to be beautiful!"

"Sorry,". I whispered as I walked away, making another note to myself about figuring out the female species.

Everyone was just there for an adventure, and we all became friends instantly with the bond of our kindred adventurous spirit. Everyone except one, that is. I had my eye on him from the beginning. I've always been able to detect a vibe, an energy that strangers emit. During our conversations, a younger kid was traveling on his own. Something was off. If he was a guitar, the strings were out of tune. If he was a photo, it would not have been in focus. And if he was a Kardashian, he would have been a Jenner.

My new nickname inside my head for this kid was "Cringy Kid". Every time he spoke, I cringed. As our conversations continued, I felt a connection with everyone except this cringy kid. And then he said something that was the most alarming and cringe of all. Somehow, we talked about pigs and bacon, and then *Cringy Kid* spoke up when he should not have.

"Did you know pigs are closely related to humans? Scientists are even trying to clone human organs in pigs. That is why I think humans would taste good, because bacon tastes so good!" The cringy kid blurted out.

My buddy Russ and I slowly turned to each other, stunned, with our eyes open wide. We didn't say it out loud, but we both communicated exactly what we were thinking.

"We have to spend the next four days with this guy alone, deep in an Amazon rainforest?!" That was the worst thing anyone could have said moments before getting on the boat with strangers.

The fireworks in my mind exploded with this statement. I mean, first, it kind of made sense. That disturbed me. I thought back to all those 4H fair booths as a kid. My favorite thing at the fair was to walk through the barnyard animals. Except for the pigs. I hated the pigs. Flies everywhere. Stupid nose. Dirty and gross. No fur, you couldn't pet them. Nothing, I mean NOTHING about a pig is appealing. Well, almost nothing. I was sorry the first day I asked Mom where bacon comes from. When she said pigs, if it had not tasted like the ascension to heaven, I would have spit out my bacon in horror.

"Mom? You mean this holy of all holy meat comes from those disgusting pigs?! How does that work?"

I thought of how bacon magically turned any food into a masterpiece. Asparagus rolled with bacon. Pancakes and bacon. Lettuce and tomato sandwich? Gross, but then add bacon? Once again, a masterpiece sandwich.

My mind flashed back to the present. "Ok, so what if this guy's comment kind of makes sense? That is NOT what you say to a group of strangers entering a rainforest."

I began alerting the defense mechanisms in my brain.

"Ok, Dave. Think. Let's see, never turn your back on him. Do not be alone with him. Always sit at the opposite ends during dinnertime."

As my mind raced on how to survive the next four days with this cannibal, the Ecuadorian guide came by again and asked, "How much chicken you like please?" Russ and I were both hungry and asked for the maximum. The cringy kid then spoke in a beta male voice to the guide. "No chicken for me, please. I don't eat meat."

Russ and I then both looked at each other and gave a tremendous sigh of relief. Oh, thank goodness, this cannibal is a vegetarian. The next four days were all the Indiana Jones I could ever hope for, and I even called the Asian blogger beautiful, once.

# THE BIGFOOT HITCHHIKER

"Missoula" was the only word written on his cardboard sign. The man holding it looked like an Old English Sheepdog with the hair color of an auburn grizzly bear which I had just seen a half hour ago. I was at Mammoth Hot Springs in Yellowstone Park, driving from my family's cabin just outside the park.

"Hey, I'm going to Missoula!" I thought.

"Well, what a coincidence. I could really help this guy out."

I didn't give it further thought, so I drove up to the stop sign he was under and rolled down the window.

"Sir, I can give you a ride to Livingston if you like?"

I was just out of college and realized I was already making smart decisions with my life. I only told him Livingston (fifty miles away) just in case he was annoying to travel with.

"Sure!" the shaggy man said and jumped in.

I think I could have said any town in Montana. My first impression was his destination was wherever he slept that night. I liked him already.

I asked why he was going to Missoula.

"I don't know." He answered as he gazed at the Montana scenery outside.

"Oookaaay…" I thought this was a little strange. This man was short of a few tools in the shed. Boy, was I proud of my street smarts at this point for only saying Livingston.

Then he pulled out a Bible from his backpack. My eyes grew cautious. There was now only a North and South Pole with this situation. No middle ground.

"Do you believe in The Bible?" He asked.

I wanted to answer, "Now? or after I drop you off and I am safe?"

He talked and dominated the conversation about his beliefs about the Bible. Coincidentally, about this time, we drove past a town called Prey, because that is exactly what I was doing. That's when the hitchhiker switched subjects like a traffic light.

"Do you believe in Bigfoot?" He asked in all sincerity.

Again, I wanted to give him the answer AFTER I dropped him off.

"I don't know. I've never seen him. Do you?"

Why did I just ask him if he's seen Bigfoot? Stupid. Stupid.

He answered, "I have…" Then gazed back at the scenery silently without giving me details.

Then he dominated the conversation again, but this time it was about Bigfoot. He started spewing fact after fact about the nature of Bigfoot.

"Why is it that sightings of Bigfoot in the Sierra Nevada only happen in the wintertime? It's because it migrates," he said with the conviction and poignancy of a college professor.

The man continued to spew out facts and make compelling arguments for the existence of Bigfoot, citing references to logging camps that were ransacked. He talked about how Bigfoots communicate with other Bigfoots with a distinct knocking on wood and then demonstrated the knock himself. He talked about how they are remnants of Gigantopithecus, an extinct ape from Asia, and how they crossed the Bering Sea.

I was captivated. This was 1996. The internet had just become a thing. How did one man know so much about Bigfoot? The man kept talking as we drove, and soon Livingston was upon us. I had so many more questions about Bigfoot that I wasn't ready for Livingston yet. I broke out of my white lie.

"Ya know, I am actually going to Bozeman. Would you like a ride there?"

I didn't want to push my luck with taking him all the way to Missoula, but I really needed at least twenty-five more miles of Bigfoot. This turned out to be one of the most fascinating conversations I had ever had.

"Sure" He replied.

Once again, I think I could have said anything or anywhere and he would have agreed to go there. So, I drove the shaggy man another twenty-five miles to Bozeman, asking even more questions.

"So, does Bigfoot have a family? How many are there? Why are they so elusive?" I was now entranced.

He took his time explaining each question like Socrates to Plato. I was now a believer—Bigfoot had to be real. I pulled into downtown Bozeman and asked where he would like to be dropped off.

"Right here is fine."

He didn't care. I should have known. He thanked me for the ride, and I wished him luck. I didn't even get his name. The shaggy hitchhiker then opened the passenger door and nearly tripped getting out of the car with what I just noticed were some rather enormous feet on this guy. "You ok? That was a close one."

"Yeah, I'm fine he said with a sheepish smile, it happens all the time."

I waved goodbye, wished him luck as he vanished into the crowd like David Copperfield, and I never saw the gentleman again.

# A SIXTH-GRADE VILLAGE IDIOT SAVANT

"You have a big nose, Mr. Fuqua!" Mr. Busch, my sixth-grade teacher, blurted at me. We were all lined up at the door, ready to go to lunch with Mr. Busch in the front. I was in the back of the line near his desk, where my test score was lying on top.

"That's a little rude," I thought to myself. I felt my nose, confused about why he would say that. I didn't think it was that big—never been called Pinocchio. I kept feeling my nose as the line moved out the door past Mr. Busch. He kept giving me a disgusted look.

"Man … why would he call my big nose out like that out of the blue?" I thought as I walked to the lunchroom while wishing I had a mirror. Maybe that is why Jodie never talked to me.

Jodi hasn't talked to me much, ever since fifth grade. During one rainy recess, I threw worms at her. Apparently, fifth-grade girls didn't recognize the love language of fifth-grade boys throwing worms at them because they liked them. That was the first time I learned to fear Mr. Busch. He was on recess duty at the time and busted me. Since it was near the end of recess, he ordered me to come into his classroom and "Assume the position!" We all know what that phrase meant. With Mr. Busch, if you got in trouble, he yelled, "Assume the position!" And you

150

would have to get down in a push-up position with arms extended and stay like that for five to fifteen minutes, depending on Mr. Busch's judicial decisions. This was 1984 when this punishment was acceptable. He also had a paddle in the closet for serious cases. But being in fifth grade, this punishment backfired. All my sixth-grade buddies were laughing at me. A fifth-grader assuming the position in his class. I really got some gangsta street cred.

It wasn't until my third bite of that famous Washington School macaroni goulash that it dawned on me.

"Oh! He was saying I was nosey because I was looking at my test score!" Now I was scared. He probably thought I was smarting off—feeling my nose as if it was big or not right in front of him. I was going to have to assume the position for sure after lunch. After lunch was always the worst time to assume the position. Especially today, we were playing Jeopardy, and I didn't want to miss Jeopardy.

After lunch, we all sat down, and Mr. Busch had all the clues written on the chalkboard and divided the class into two teams. He said nothing about my big nose, so he must have gotten over it. Mr. Busch was tough, but he had some great games. He put a twist on his Jeopardy game. If you got the answer right, you could step up to a line about six feet away from an empty garbage can with a wiffle softball. If you made a basket with the ball from behind the line, you got a bonus point—and I had a plan.

I just got done watching Michael Jordan jump from the free throw line during a slam dunk contest. The question was a brain teaser. If TEAM equals MEAT, then what does DAD equal?

I raised my hand as high as I could and even made grunting noises. I knew it. He called on every kid first but me and they all gave the wrong answer. I forced his hand, and I think his eyes rolled.

"Dave? Do you know the answer?"

"DAD," is the answer!

I was right. (I'll let you figure that out on your own).

I took the plastic wiffle ball and used the same abstract thinking to figure out an easy way to get the bonus point. Telling no one my plans, I walked back to the end of the room, staring at the masking tape six feet in front of the garbage can. I took off as fast as I could, running past all my classmate's puzzled looks. I made sure I didn't scratch and jumped from the masking tape with my legs spread, doing my best Michael Jordan imitation. Before I landed on the ground, I slammed the wiffle ball in the garbage can for the bonus point. There was no roar from the crowd but a single cackle from my best friend Dave, who about fell over laughing.

Mr. Busch started to say it.

"Fuqua! Assu—," but then stopped and sighed. It was Friday. Maybe he was tired. His usually authoritarian voice dropped to an exhausted, defeated middle-of-the-year schoolteacher. He even let the point stand.

"Ok, new rule," he said with his palm covering his face, "No more jumping from the free throw line like Michael Jordan."

I leaned back in my chair, relieved I didn't get in trouble, and I felt lucky to have Mr. Busch as a teacher. I scanned the room and noticed Jodie was now looking at me a little differently—with a smile. She is so lucky it's not raining today.

# THE HAIR THAT DIDN'T CARE

"That has got to be a Guinness Book of World Records!" I thought to myself as I stood in the Subway line directly behind this elderly gentleman while staring at his ears. It was a forest. Like one of those animal blankets you get at the flea market. I have never seen more hair on anyone's ears than the hair on this elderly man's ears. This included that wolfman family from South America I saw on the Discovery Channel. This man has achieved what I have been looking for my entire life. This man had zero cares left, and I could not have been more jealous!

At some point, this man must have looked in the mirror one morning with his razor in his hand. He must have looked at the tired wrinkles below his eyes as he remembered every overtime shift, every terrible boss, and every bill he had to pay. He must have looked at his thinning gray hair and remembered every time his heart was broken. He must have remembered every bully who pushed him to the ground and every time a good friend let him down. There must have been a point in which he looked at the mirror and noticed the hair accumulating on those rabbit ears of his and with a razor in hand he said to himself in the mirror, "Ya know what, I don't care anymore!" and put the razor down. His wife was standing right in front of him. Surely, she would have said something about those ears. But even she could not have control over him anymore. He was completely FREE!

I stared more at those ears as we moved closer to the foot-long toasted turkey avocado. I could not take my eyes off his ears.

"Oh, what freedom this man must have!" I thought more to myself.

He must now be the happiest man in the world. I would give anything to have that kind of freedom. This man must walk around town floating on clouds, not having to care anymore. I remembered as a kid seeing cartoon drawings of an old Wiseman up on the mountain that had all the answers. I realized now that all the depictions of the old wise man were wrong because none of those Wiseman had this much hair on their ears!

It was soon his turn to order his sandwich.

"What would you like to have today, sir?" The Subway artist asked.

He replied, "I don't care, whatever you want." In a slightly grumpy tone.

His wife piped up and interrupted like she had done this many times before. "He will have the club. American Cheese."

I admired the nirvana this man had achieved. He did not even care what sandwich he ordered. Meanwhile, my order had to be just perfect. This man truly did not care. My jealousy grew.

The next morning, I looked at my tired eyes in the mirror. The bags under my eyes were fuller than usual. I stared at my aging self a little longer with my razor next to the sink. Suddenly, the bags under my eyes temporarily disappeared as my astonished eyes grew larger.

"Oh, no!" I thought to myself, "What's that hair doing on my ear?!"

It happens. Sometimes I wake up and one of those wild hairs has grown magically overnight. I immediately remembered my hero from the day before as I stared at my razor next to my bathroom sink. My heart sank as I reached and picked up my razor.

"Dang it!" I said to myself while bringing my hand with those blades to the wild hair, "I still care."

# DOGGONE BIOLOGY LESSONS

"What's the matter Pepsi?" I whispered to my dog. I went to play in my backyard with her, but she was acting differently from normal. Pepsi was some kind of Glendivian mutt terrier thing. A great dog, but if she wasn't leashed, she would chase a few cars and we might not receive our mail that day.

Today, she wasn't interested in the tennis ball like she usually was, but a bit more concerned. I then heard a loud "Yip!" and strong panting. I looked in that direction and saw the nose of a miniature collie poking through our white picket fence, desperately trying to get in. On the other end of our backyard was another lab that I remembered belonged to a house a block away. It was vehemently pacing back and forth and scratching at the fence.

Then suddenly, Corky the poodle from across the street arrived. I could hear the first few chords of Beethoven's fifth being played as I saw that poodle's face. Dun-dun-dun-DUNN!

"Oh, no … not Corky. I hate that dog," I mumbled to myself, remembering every time Corky would bark at me and chase me down the block on my Star Wars banana seat bike.

Corky joined the other neighborhood dogs who all paced and stared in my backyard at Pepsi like she was Miss America. I ran back inside and shouted, "Mom! Every dog in the neighborhood is trying to get in our backyard! We are being attacked!"

Mom jumped up. "Gads! Get Pepsi inside now!"

I scurried and grabbed Pepsi and brought her inside. That's when Mom gave me a biology lesson. Something about not getting hit with a spade while nuder or you will be in heat.

"And whatever you do!" Mom added, "Do not let those dogs get to Pepsi!"

A couple of days later, I was carrying my trombone home from school. My band teacher didn't tell me how heavy a trombone would be for a fifth grader, and it was during those walks home I wished I had chosen the flute. After switching that trombone from sore arm to sore arm, I was finally only a couple blocks away from my house when my world changed. There, in Mrs. Olson's yard by the baseball field, was Pepsi.

"How did Pepsi get out?" I murmured to myself.

"Pepsi! Pepsi! Come here!" but Pepsi just stood there motionless.

It was like she was out of it. I walked a little faster as I mumbled, "This little dog is going to cause me a lot of trouble," in my best Luke Skywalker voice.

Then, I looked up. I froze like a statue, except for the shiver that ran down my spine. There in the middle of the street were two eyes gazing at me. It was Corky!

"No! Not Corky! Anything but Corky!" The theme to The Good, The Bad, and The Ugly played in my head.

"wahhh Wa wahhh…"

We were in a stare-down. Each calculating our next move. I hated fifth-grade math word problems, but I had to think fast.

"Hmm … let's see … if a Poodle was a hundred yards away from a dog in heat and a fifth grader carrying a trombone was an opposite seventy-five yards away, how many more little Pepsi's would there be in two months?"

But while I was doing math in my head, Corky dashed toward Pepsi and had the advantage.

I yelled out a slow motion "Nooooo! Not Corky!"

I dropped the trombone to pick up speed, but it was too late. Corky had beat me to Pepsi. I then learned another biology lesson. Pepsi looked at me helplessly. Lock and key, hand and glove, seat and belt. It was too late. I was crying. Pepsi was crying. Corky seemed just fine.

"Oh Pepsi, what have I done?! I'm so sorry … I'm so sorry…" I screamed as I fell next to my trombone and looked up at the spinning sky above me. "Not Corky … Not Corky…"

The tears filled my eyes. I wished they had filled my ears. That night I played the sad slow notes of 'Taps' on my trombone over and over.

"Stop playing that song!" my mom yelled from downstairs.

"She won't be saying that two months from now," I mumbled.

Two months later, in the same room where I played Taps, Mom delivered five healthy puppies, not knowing who the father was.

I knew.

But I was too embarrassed to tell anyone. I couldn't let my friends know my dog had babies with Corky. Gross.

A few months later, we gave away all the puppies except one who looked just like her mother. Not long after, Pepsi finally accomplished her dream of catching a Chevrolet and we started to receive mail again. With the vacancy, Pepsi II now found herself a permanent home. My oldest brother Eric had just started to pheasant hunt and decided to find out if a half-poodle and half-Glendivian mutt terrier would make a good hunting dog.

An amazing thing happened. I can only imagine the first time Michael Jordon dribbled a basketball or Wayne Gretzky put on skates.

This dog, whom I can't even say the father's name anymore, turned out to be the most amazing pheasant dog anyone has ever seen.

My brother would take him with his hunting friend's expensive, highly trained dogs. Pepsi II would outperform all of them. He just might have been the best, smartest dog our family has ever had.

Thanks, Cor— Thanks, Cor—

I'm sorry, I still can't say his name.

Thanks, poodle from across the street!

# THAT'S WHAT COWBOYS DO

"Because that's what cowboys do!" My friend snapped back as I asked yet another rodeo question. By this time, he was sorry he invited me, but I just witnessed Chet, who weighed maybe a buck fifty, get his chaps handed to him by falling from a fifteen-hundred-pound bucking bronc named Elmer. I watched Chet hobble back to the gate.

"So, they made that bronc buck on purpose? And Chet rode that because why?"

Even though I was born and raised in a state in which cows outnumber humans by over two to one, I knew nothing about ranch life. I felt like a blond watching football. Puzzled at how this sport is so popular, I asked again.

"So, you are telling me these cowboys do this every night? He can barely walk. He just gets up and does it all over again?"

My friend once again replied, "That's what Cowboys do." in a way that Google translates 'cowboy' to mean, 'stop talking'.

The next event was steer wrestling. They would give these little calves a head start, make them think they had a chance, and then a few seconds later, a "Half-Nelson" wrestling move brought them mercilessly to the ground. It was just like having an older brother. This event I understood all too well, but from the calf's point of view.

Then they set up three barrels in some sort of Bermuda triangle arrangement. Seeing all those barrels gave me another older brother flashback. My older brother once told me to call my seventh-grade English teacher "Darryl the Barrel" because he was shaped like a barrel.

The next morning, I passed by my teacher and with a confident naïve Brady Bunch smile on my face yelled, "Hey, Darryl the Barrel!"

I arrived home late after school that day because of some detention and the first thing I did was go right to my brother.

"Hey! You said to call my teacher Darrel the Barrel! I got detention!"

"Well, duh, not to his face!" my brother replied, laughing.

My attention returned as suddenly as the gates burst open and a young cowgirl on a horse shot out like David Copperfield. She then circled each barrel at a dizzying pace and raced back like her barn was on fire. Then, like Amelia Earhart, she disappeared forever. I was so confused; it happened so fast. Why did she do that? Where did she go? Where did she come from? Over and over, horses with cowgirls would dart from nowhere, do a few circles, and dart back to whatever world they came from.

Once the barrels were cleared and the riding girls disappeared, next came two friends swinging ropes like I used to see Wonder Woman do when I was a kid. The two friends would chase a calf running for its quarter-pounder life when within seconds the first friend would toss his magic Wonder Woman rope around its horns and the next friend around the calf's legs. The two horses then backed up, and the calf stretched like a medieval king had sentenced it to the rack.

"Do we have any veterans in the stands today?" the announcer proudly asked.

One by one, audience members began popping up. Older bodies with a slight hunch, one could see the years of labor done with their own

161

hands, as they now stood erect with perfect posture. I couldn't help but notice the number of flags around the arena that bore the same colors of these cowboys' bruises and perhaps a star for each one. The crowd then cheered the loudest I have heard yet.

"They sure are patriotic at these rodeos, aren't they?" I commented to my friend.

"That's what cowboys do!" He replied in a way that once again told me to shut up and just watch.

Next came the bull riding. Everyone was waiting for this. Ironically, the same amount of time I take to eat one of them is the magic amount of time required to stay on them. Eight seconds. To make things more interesting, I asked my buddy if he wanted to place a five-dollar bet on who would win, and to keep me quiet, he agreed.

Knowing nothing, I looked at the names of the bull riders on the ticket. Hank, Chet, Brandt, Tate, Lane and Morgan.

"Morgan!" I thought, "What kind of blue state, two-syllable cowboy name is Morgan?"

Easy money. "I bet you five to one Morgan does not win!"

Just to shut me up, my friend agreed. Each bull reacted and spun differently, like an F5 tornado. The bull's only goal was to knock off the cowboy before the horn blew and vice versa for the cowboy, as every one of them hobbled back after their ride.

Each bull had a name. If they gave me a chance to name a bull, I'd simply name it "Life".

The bull riding ended, and I had to ask my friend one more question as he sat back down with his new free drink.

"So, these guys just go from rodeo to rodeo, day after day, even after getting bucked off and beat up like that?"

My friend, with his free drink in hand, replied in a more attentive tone this time.

"You see, Dave, that's why these things are so patriotic. Just like in the USA, it doesn't matter how many times we get bucked off, hurt, broken bones, or bruised. We will always get back on the horse. *That's what cowboys do!*"

# THE PRICE TO SKIP SCHOOL IS RIGHT, BOB

"Mom, I have a sore throat! I can't go to school today." I wasn't even faking this time. Even so, staying home sick in 1981 was a tough sell.

"Oh, you are fine!" She replied.

I was prepared for this answer. Every '80's mom vied for that coveted attendance record for their child. It meant that you were a much better parent if your child won the school attendance record. Every day, there was quiet time after the second recess. However, it was never quiet. Especially during those cold winter months, it was always a symphony of sniffling and coughing. I had to sit in front of Travis, who had won Best Attendance two years in a row. Travis was also a walking Halls commercial. Nothing could penetrate his stuffy nose. Only a hospital stay could keep Travis home from school; a sure sign of great parenting.

I thought for a moment, "Do I really want to be sick today?" It wasn't bowling or Cub Scout night. The rule was if I was too sick for school, I was too sick to do anything after school. It was Wednesday, piano lessons day. Oh, I was definitely going to be sick. I quickly drummed up a few coughs to help sell my sickness to Mom. She let out a sigh.

"OK, but NO TV!" she said, hoping that would ease her conscience about being a terrible parent and losing that attendance award. I nodded my head yes, knowing she would be at work soon.

Dad ran to the store real quick to buy a liter of Coke and 7up. This was our usual go-to medicine in 1981.

I stayed in bed until I heard the doors shut and knew I had the house to myself. Ahhh. A day of self-quarantining had its perks. I ran straight to the TV and sat close enough to turn the dial with my feet. The remote control would not be in our household until the following year.

As life changing as the remote was, it was also the source of many wars in a household of six kids. My siblings and I would fight over the remote like it was Frodo and Gollum fighting over the ring.

"My Precious! My Precious!"

Whoever held the remote possessed the power of a thousand kings and the keys to the universe. But today was my day. I had a liter of Coke and seven hours of self-isolation, and it was glorious.

I knew my sick day routine. My foot moved the dial over to PBS. Sesame Street, Mr. Rodgers then The Price is Right. Three hours of pure entertainment bliss. How my parents survived growing up without four TV channels, I will never know. I poured myself a Coke to ease my sore throat and let the party begin!

Sesame Street was brought to us by the letter B. I thought of different ways Ernie could drive that annoying obsessive-compulsive Bert crazy with things that started with B. I was kind of hoping for a baseball bat.

Oh, then there was Snuffleupagus! Will Big Bird finally get to reveal his friend?

"Oh, C'mon! Gordon missed him again! How do you not see a wooly mammoth on a New York Street?"

Next up was Mr. Roger's Neighborhood, but ya know, I was nine years old by now, and honestly, Mr. Rogers was creeping me out. I moved the dial with my foot over to CBS. It was Alice. Alice liked to say "Kiss my grits!" all the time and the entire world would laugh. I had no idea what grits were, but it didn't matter. The greatest show of all time was on next—the Holy of Holies—the crème de la crème. It was the whole reason for staying home from school. The Price is Right! Nothing satisfied a 1981 sick day like The Price is Right. "Oh, please, oh, please, have the Cliffhangers game today!" I thought. Sure enough, it was my lucky sick day.

"Yodelaloo. Yadallayoo. Yodallayalloooo. Yadalaloo…" Every 1980s kid knows exactly what I am talking about. Will the cardboard mountain climber fall off the mountain free-falling to his mortal death, or will the contestant win a vacuum? It was so darned exciting. I never understood why Bob Barker always asked us to get our pets nuder. Pets are already nude. Bob was creeping me out too.

After the Price is Right, my foot turned the dial to ABC where Family Feud was on. Why does this host kiss every female contestant?

Suddenly, Bob Barker and Mr. Rogers didn't seem so creepy anymore. This guy takes the cake. After Family Feud, the high of a self-isolated sick day went flat like my medicated Coca-Cola. It was all soap operas. Soap operas compounded my sore throat with cabin fever.

It wasn't long before I realized cabin fever was way worse than a sore throat. I turned off the TV with my foot and wandered over to the window. I gazed at my Star Wars banana seat bike and stared dreamily at my basketball hoop, thinking of all my friends at school. I didn't want to stay home by myself anymore, and I didn't know when my sore throat would get better, but I knew it would, eventually.

A couple of days later, I felt better. I jumped on my Star Wars bike, but it felt different now. The joy of riding was so much sweeter than it was before. Basketball was sweeter, and playing with my friends was sweeter. Everything I once loved was so much sweeter and appreciated than it was before. The Price is Right was furthest from my mind. I looked back and realized how glad I was for being miserable for just a few days. Without the misery, I would have never realized how joyous the things I love are.

You can't put a price on that, Bob!

# Bonus Stories! (The next three are a little different)

# THE FIRE KEEPER

A long time ago, there was this village in a cold northern region. It had been cold for centuries. In the middle of the town, lay a large fire pit filled with a tower of wood. Despite being intended for a large fire, no one knew how to light it. Then one stormy day something happened that was the most unexpected. Lighting struck the woodpile and POOF—a large fire emitted. Everyone in the town cheered and gathered around. They had never felt such warmth before. They danced around the fire and continued to dance throughout the night, as this had never been seen in their dark village before. But slowly the fire got lower and lower.

"We need a fire keeper!" the mayor said. "Who can I entrust to keep this fire going? This is the most important job in the village. We need this fire going!"

The crowd stayed silent. It was too much of a responsibility, and the fire was too important to the town. They were all too scared to take the job. The mayor asked again and finally, a young man shouted, "I will!"

The mayor agreed, and the young man was now called the Master Fire Keeper. The fire keeper quickly gathered up as much wood as he could from the forest. He stacked the wood on all at once and the fire then grew to a raging height. Ashes fell on the homes nearby and came close to burning them down. The fire was too hot for anybody to stay near it. "Not so much wood!" The mayor yelled at the kid. "You will burn the whole place down!" The young fire keeper learned quickly. The fire burned fine for a while and the fire keeper was feeling confident. But then he got complacent. He stopped feeding it wood and took a long nap. The fire keeper woke up just in time, as the fire was almost out! He quickly gathered some more wood and realized his mistake. He thought to himself, "I can't stop gathering wood. I must really work at this. I can't let it get too small, and I can't let it get too big."

For months and days, the village had a beautiful fire. The fire keeper was happy and so was the village. They considered him a hero.

"I could do this job forever," the fire keeper said to himself.

He loved making people happy. But then it started raining. The fire keeper worked as hard as he could to keep the fire going. All day he gathered wood, but the rains kept coming and the fire went lower and lower.

"No! Please, please don't go fire!" he begged, but the rain kept coming.

Eventually, the fire went out and the fire keeper cried.

"I did everything I could do! It's not fair!"

Even the village stopped giving him praise. Some thought it was his fault and gave him dirty looks. The mayor came over and put his arm around the young fire keeper.

"Don't worry, it wasn't your fault at all," the mayor said.

"What are we going to do?" the fire keeper asked with wet eyes.

"Don't worry," the mayor replied in an experienced tone.

"Lighting will strike again."

# VIC-TIMS AND VIC-TORS

Here is a tale of the King of Vic and his two twin princes. Prince Tim and Prince Tor, both have the same appearances.

Each prince was very opposite in their own way. Tor left the castle as a young lad to experience the world far away, but Tim was scared and stayed.

The land under the rule of King Vic fared well enough, but his time had come as he grew old and weary. Due to Tor's absence, his son Tim assumed control of the Kingdom of Vic, causing unease among the people.

Now, the Vic Tims, as the people of the land were called under Tim's rule, were alarmed. You see, Prince Tim was given everything to him as a boy. The old ways of hard work had become a blur.

The Vic Tims complained, "We can't farm because of all the rocks in the field! Now we can't feed the village, not with our yield!"

"And we durst not build a pleasant house. The dragon will breathe fire and we have no more water to douse!"

Thus, the land of Vic gradually turned to shambles, and the Vic Tims all pointed to each other, ready to assault.

"It's your fault! No, it's your fault! It's the king's fault! It's the dragon's fault! It's not MY fault!"

One by one, Vic Tim after Vic Tim quit their jobs in the land of Vic. The only way this town will get better is to point the blame, they thought. That's the trick!

Meanwhile, season after season, fewer crops were tilled, and fewer homes were built, yet nobody knew the reason.

King Vic Tim looked out across his shattered land. He couldn't understand how his town just fell. It must be, he thought, after all, he put every penny into a wishing well.

But then one day came a visitor to the town of Vic Tims gates. The guards thought he looked like their King Vic Tim, only with much more grace.

They now recognized him as it was their ol' Prince Tor! Raise the gates for the Vic Tor!

The prince and his stallion trotted through his brother's land, but he could hardly take any more.

"What happened to our magnificent land?" the astonished Vic Tor asked the Vic Tims. They all pointed fingers, but no finger was pointed at themselves.

The Victims rambled on with excuses on their list. Too many dragons, too many rocks, and many more excuses, they exclaimed with fists raised. Tor then gave a wink, and the smile on his face grew, for his travels taught him a world he wished these Vic Tims knew.

"You have dragons!" he exclaimed, "This is great news!"

The Vic Tims gave Vic Tor a nasty look. They were not amused.

"I have been to so many dark and cold cities with no fire or light. This is a great opportunity to gain warmth and sight in the night!"

The Vic Tims gave Vic Tor a puzzled look.

"That sounds just fine, but how will you do that? The dragons burn our houses every time!"

Tor went on, "You have rocks in the field you say? This is great news. We can build rock homes and chimneys. Let's start today!

"When the dragons breathe their fire, we shall put wood on the stacks. Our stone homes will be protected, yet the fire and light will be kept intact. Then the rocks will be gone and the soil ready to harvest, leaving plenty of grain for us and all the rest.

"We can bring this town back if we set our minds right. Just think positive, work hard and we will win this fight."

Some of the older Vic Tims gave Vic Tor a blank stare. They didn't like change and thought Vic Tor was full of hot air. But some of the young Vic Tims were ready for change. They believed Vic Tor and their lives had rearranged. These young Vic Tims then asked for less and worked more. They pointed their fingers at themselves and called each other Vic Tors!

They did not accuse each other of fault. They worked hard and stood tall. Soon the town changed and it bared fruit for them all!

And King Vic Tim, well, he took the praise for all his kingdom's success. He threw more pennies on the wishing well, for that must be the reason he thought for all that he's blessed.

# GLADYS AND VIXEN

"Meow … meow … rharr … meow" Gladys, the little old lady that lived by herself, heard it over and over in the alley behind her. She looked out the window and heard it again.

"Meow … meow!" the frail cat cried over and over.

Gladys put on her robe and slippers and walked over to the shy cat in the alley. She could tell it hadn't had food for days. It had a few scratches on its head and some of its ribs were showing.

"Oh, you poor thing!" Gladys said and tried to pick it up.

"Rahrr!" The cat snapped at her.

"Ok, Ok." Gladys talked in a sweet tone to it, "It's ok, I won't hurt you."

She could tell the cat did not trust her for a minute, so she went back inside and opened a can of tuna to bring to her. The cat was still shy but would never turn away a can of tuna and darted for the can. Gladys tried to pet the cat again while it was eating and then, "Rahhrr!"

The cat gave a little hiss at the one who fed it. The previous owner would always hurt the cat while it was eating, before it was abandoned, so the cat didn't trust anyone.

"Now, now kitty. It's going to be ok. I won't hurt you." She said as she walked into the house.

For several days, the cat kept coming back to Gladys's house and Gladys being lonely since her husband died a few years ago, always looked forward to feeding it. A few weeks passed, and Gladys was always faithful with a can of tuna. Then one day, the cat followed Gladys back to her home. A sweet "meow" came from the cat instead of the usual angry "Rahrr!"

"Do you want to come inside, kitty?" Gladys asked in the sweetest voice.

The cat replied with an even sweeter, "Meow!".

"Oh, aren't you the sweetest thing? I think I will name you Vixen!" Gladys could not have been happier to have some company, and Vixen could not have been happier to have a home.

Gladys and Vixen, for the next few weeks, became very comfortable with each other. Vixen would even let Gladys pet her, but only after she got her tuna.

One day, after Vixen got her tuna, she sat by Gladys to let her pet her while she watched TV. Vixen remembered the last home she was in. The home she grew up in. Her owners were always yelling at her. Sometimes they would kick her for no reason. It was what she knew growing up. Gladys was so sweet and full of love. She always talked in a sweet voice to Vixen and Vixen felt uncomfortable. She became suspicious. There has to be something wrong here. Humans do not talk in a sweet, loving voice all the time.

Vixen feared getting abandoned again. This was too good to be true. So, one night, after her tuna, as Gladys began petting her, she bit her!

"Ow! What did you do that for Vixen?" Gladys screamed as she started crying, running to get a band-aid.

Vixen darted and hid under a chair. As far as Vixen knew, she was just protecting herself. It didn't feel right for her to be treated so well. Something was going to happen to her, so she had to bite first.

Gladys let it go and kept feeding Vixen her daily tuna. Gladys was very consistent. She never missed a day. It was so consistent; that Vixen felt uneasy. It wasn't what she was used to. Something bad was about to happen. Vixen just knew it. Just like her whole life, nothing lasts forever. With each day that Gladys gave all the food and attention Vixen could ever ask for, Vixen became wearier. Then, completely out of the blue Vixen, bit Gladys again. Vixen believed it was her or Gladys. "Ow!" Gladys screamed in pain again as she put a bandage on the bloody wound.

Gladys cried as she said, "You are just going to have to go, Vixen. I can't be hurt anymore."

The cat knew it all along. Vixen was right, after all. It was too good to be true and out she ran to the alley where she felt most comfortable. Vixen went from garbage can to garbage can, feeling sorry for herself.

"I must be the unluckiest cat in the world," Vixen thought to herself.

After days of scrounging from garbage can to garbage can, an owner caught her snooping around.

"Scram! Get out of here!" and Vixen darted off.

The next day, Vixen went back to the same garbage can. Again, the owner had some leftover chicken wings in the garbage that got Vixen's attention. She quietly snuck up to the can and peeked inside, using her paws to search. Just then, a broom smacked her face.

"Didn't I tell you to, Scram!" the owner of the garbage can said as Vixen did a flip off the garbage but still landed on her feet. Vixen then gave a soft "Meow!" as the garbage can owner looked at her with hands planted on his hips.

"Ok, fine, you want a home, then get in here!" he said as he threw a couple of bones in a dish by his porch.

"One wrong move and it will be more than a broom next time!"

So, the garbage can owner let Vixen live on his front porch, but never inside. Now and then he would throw some chicken bones at her and maybe some dry food. He always yelled to Vixen, "Get over here, ya stupid cat!" and Vixen would come running. The cat felt comfortable now, for this is what she was used to. She never left the old man for the rest of her life. Occasionally, she would get a broom to the face or the butt just for trying to come inside, but she never left the porch to find another home.

The cat did not have to worry about somebody like Gladys kicking her to the streets someday now. That pain would have been just too much. This is where she belonged. This is where Vixen felt comfortable. The old man continued to swear and curse at her.

"You dumb cat! Get over here!"

Vixen would never bite this man; after all, he could never hurt her like Gladys could. A broom to the face did not hurt after all. It just meant the old man cared, and that Vixen was loved. The old man and Vixen lived ever after.

# ABOUT DINODAVE

Dave "Dinodave" Fuqua was born and raised in the small town of Glendive Montana in an era when childhood freedom was a gift of rambunctious adventures. Dave acquired his name "Dinodave" because of his knack for finding dinosaurs.

Glendive is surrounded by badlands, where Dave often spends his free time exploring and prospecting for fossils. He graduated from Montana State University with a Biology degree and has recently taught high school for the last three years. Dave writes a column for the Ranger Review monthly and previously had his very own morning radio show on KDXN in Glendive.

Today, he spends his free time making videos for his YouTube channel and playing tennis when he is not out looking for dinosaurs. His favorite moments in paleontology were going to Mongolia on a dig with famed paleontologist Jack Horner and being featured in the Dutch TV series "Dinojacht".

You can follow him and his dinosaur adventures on YouTube at Dinodave Paleo Adventures (dinodaveadventures.com/all-new-dinodave-adventure-videos). Ride along and reminisce with the pot-pourri of amazing, humorous, heartfelt short stories presented in a way that only Dinodave can do.

www.ingramcontent.com/pod-product-compliance
Lightning Source LLC
LaVergne TN
LVHW011329080426
835513LV00006B/256